northern wild roses / deth interrupts th dansing

bill bissett

bill bissett

talonbooks
vancouver

Talonbooks
P.O. Box 2076, Vancouver, British Columbia, Canada V6B 3S3
www.talonbooks.com

Typeset in Librarian and printed and bound in Canada.

First Printing: 2005

Library and Archives Canada Cataloguing in Publication

Bissett, Bill, 1939–
    Northern wild roses : deth interrupts th dansing / Bill Bissett.

Poems.
ISBN 0-88922-532-X

    I. Title.

PS8503.I78N67 2005   C811'.54   C2005-902475-5

The publisher gratefully acknowledges the financial support of the Canada Council for the Arts; the Government of Canada through the Book Publishing Industry Development Program; and the Province of British Columbia through the British Columbia Arts Council for our publishing activities.

Canada Council   Conseil des Arts
for the Arts   du Canada

Canada

big thanks 2

vallum rampike matrix   criminal cabinet   fiddlehead
th small cities book unarmd spire wher sum uv thees
works first apeerd

sum uv thees texts ar availabul with sounds n mewsik
on **deth interrupts th dansing / a strangr space** cd
from red deer press with **pete dako** composr mastr uv
mixing audio artist n musician   doktor bedlows inam
orata i cud reed a blank envelope 2 yu eye met him in
xcelsior   whn i herd yu call me wayze uv th deep time
on our hands well if it isint   sew we wer sittin a round
talkin talkin   sew much thanks 2 **pete dako** n **ambrose
pottie** percussyun n **red deer press** n **talonbooks** 4
making ths all possibul

trust he sd 2 me

in th godesses n gods
who made us howevr

intrpretid all thees flowings
flowrings my bodee   thn

shining in th suddn
hedlites turning 2 see

our eyez meeting his
th drivrs n mine he

pulls in stops i get in
n we ar sew off n

th stars n moon
spin n dance

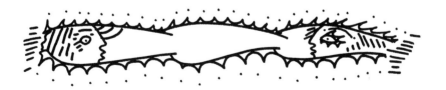

sumtimes th world

with all its binaree warring problematiks n sew
impondrabul komplexiteez is gratefulee not
with us n ther can b

such glowing sumthing amayzing almost happend
i thot th day b4

ther may b infinit impondrabuls love on all uv
them gold faeree dust sprinkling on them all
th empress told me

th alchemee uv th transformativizing modules
on theyr own kontinualing changing leeping 2 nu
platforms uv being

th endless ocean uv memoree n time all parts uv
each othr infinitlee folding in2 each othr n sew
dispersing infinitlee simultaneouslee all such
glowing

i hope iul always remembr longs thers memoree
dont yu think uv whn a lovd wun visits n thers
cinnamon dansing in yr hed n th glowing

from th peopul n my paintings at th pteros art
galleree th art opning n all th loves th glowing n
th beautiful n surprizing ice storm michel n jona
than navigatid us thru th long streets we all rockd
thru 2 get 2 we wer all inside virginia n randee
waiting embrayzing lites on sumthing amayzing
did happn in th beautiful pteros art galleree all

th glowing

whos wings fold ovr us leed us
in2   purpul dreems

i cud reed a blank envelope 2 yu

n tell yu abt th toy peopul   i cud reed a blank
envelope 2 yu n tell yu all abt th toy peopul in th toy
cars hauntid by th free way all th hauntid peopul
in th toy cars looking 4 th free way looking 4 th
free way free way turning th book turning th pages
                                        i cud tell yu abt
  all th hauntid peopul in th hauntid cars surroundid
by th free wayze   all th toy peopul in th toy cars
  wanting 4   th free waay   is it heer is it ther is it
ovr ther   deep within   as sew manee say   all th toy
                            peopul in th
hauntid cars hauntid by th free way all th hauntid
 peopul in th
  toy cars   surroundid by   th free wayze   wanting 2
make it
          wanting 2 find it wanting 2 score   wanting
mor n mor n mor   toy peopul cummin home 2 toy
pooduls th toy peopul   in th toy cars   sew hauntid
     did yu see th moon   moov thru th sky
     did u see th moon   moov thru yr eye
      did yu see th moon   eet th sky did yu see th
moon eet u n i th moon   eet all th toy peopul in
th toy cars looking 4 th free way th toy pooduls wait
ing 4 them
                on   th free way
          looking 4 th free   wayze
            th free wayze   all th
            toy peopul   in th
                toy   cars

8

we dansd   sew   goldn

n we dansd silvr   til th stars fell
  all ovr th erth   n th moon sang
   in our lives

       that cello song

dew yu remembr
dew yu remembr   was it onlee last nite

we dansd in th sky   th nites in th eye uv
time laffing n laffing   hard spaces we live
thru as if we cud onlee sumtimes heer all
 ths smiling all ths smiling
         th ocean hauls
byond our moods has its own moovs 2 make
touches us our strange psycholojeez n
 reptilian foldings disapeer karessing
whales tidal beeches evreewher
          n we dansd
n we dansd embraysing kissing n glide
  n turn   yr turning
  uv yr eye   eye

yu slide yr fingrs in2 my glands lokate th
ships uv dreems apeer thru th wheet fields th
jazz uv th citee holding th torches sail thru
th mirage n echoez uv times dew yu remembr
dew yu remembr th billowee vastness sound
 ing th waves ekstatik aves bring us sew
achinglee in2 th prcussiv deep n f l y

dew yu remembr   was it onlee
  dew yu remembr   last nite

dansing   can stall deth

nowun is rite   yu ar not rite   i am not rite
sew far th ocean is always veree big veree wet
n can caws drowning   unless our lungs wer
diffrentlee konstruktid   ar yu dansing yet

yu can worree why he didint arriv why he lied why
shes gone missing agen why yu have not
found trew love n maybe dont reelee want that
agen or dew yu   r yu dansing now

yu can wundr what effekt what yu want can have
on what happns aneeway wud yu like sum mor t
dew yu heer th mewsik yu can obsess n get sew
sad from all ths yr frend phoning in verbal abuse
frends calling in love sew fine yu jump up play
swamperella   we dont have answrs   we cant know
aneething 2 much we ar sophistikatid n literate
kreetshurs full uv longing we can keel ovr with
sadness sumtimes who isint missing from sumwun
pray 4 xcellent storeez n a levl uv being byond anee
storee get up n moov yr feet moov yr arms go
round th room go thru th room why keel yet   b
we can rock

in th moon rooms snow n blizzard winds howling
out ther dansing interrupts deth yes th beet keeps
on rockin hands keep on klapping yr bodee feels
all th work wev askd it 2 dew releeses its joy its
ardour not dour fidduls cats in th moon howling
moord dansing in infinit erth rooms

did xcellent things happn bcoz we made them or
bcoz we leefs f let them wch proporsyuns we nevr
know b th terrain is deep labyrintheean n
missing from us n its self   fles lefs th elfin kern
els neandrthals have bin reveeld as not our
ancestors erthlings ar we orphand in space n
time lost n sew belonging   endlesslee heer

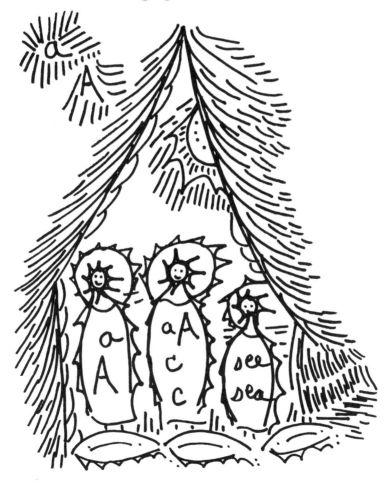

singing voices from th hiway from th pine
treez smell th bereez fir its a brave dreem
we can b th lite n th dark

uv kours we keep giving our hearts wch
cawses us 2 b hauntid by anxieteez with
holdings strangelee sleepless nites whn

all about dinasaurs

hegel containrs 4
kontradicksyuns

dont have always
2 answr th phone

2 chek on th
flying mountin

ther is
no way

out uv love

(th) system is
not (a) masheen

let that wun
figur yu out

have yu tried
just feeling

th love
flow

thru myself
alone b th

love burn

sumtimes th feelings

swell   sumtimez th
feelings know what
they can know

2 say 2 yu okay

dew yu want 2
cum 2 th meeting
up on th hill

wev cum back 2
sing 4 th erth

dew yu want 2
hold my heart
in yrs 4 a whil
th sky goez on
4evr

n evr n evr n evr
n evr n evr n evr
n evr n evr n evr

n wer dansing 4
th sky

wer dansing 4 th rivrs

th rivrs uv th erth ar

th rivrs uv our hearts

i think yu knew ths alredee tho

sew 2 recap n thn suddnlee a swift wind fastr n
fullr thn aneewun cud imagine moovd thru th
treez on th othr side uv th barn th great barn
doors startid klakking we surelee cud heer as
well th xasperatid neighing uv th horses inside th
barn a hauntid human vois sew almost
skreeming above th low moon konsidrablee
startuld   we raced out th door may b not th
britest thing 2 dew at that wretchid time n saw
giant treez   th wuns ovr by th neer medow yu
know hurtuling thru th sky th ship was cum
ming 4 us agen

xcellent i sd its abt time n we rushd hedlong 2
bord get away from th dismal human specees
n theyr war like wayze 2 predominant sew
disgusting not evreewun not evn th majoritee

but thees old binaree wayze kontributing 2 unin
formd powr dreems n criminal ambishyuns n
mass killings its all murdr whatevr peopul try 2
kall it on all sides now who cud stop it we cud
not take it aneemor n soon we wud b in th ship
taking off geting out n luckee n sew grateful they
had cum 4 us 2 a galaxee wher beings wer not
afrayd uv tendrness imaginaysyun   hoped now
we wud nevr cum back 2 erth it was 2 heart brek
ing 2 b among anee mor n hedid as fast as we cud
tord anothr galaxee wheww we tuk a fast look b

hind whol citeez n towns wer blowing up th fire
works uv deth sew bhind us sew disapointing n
cud b a nitemare memoree 4 a veree long time
i wish our specees cud get bettr if i wish hard
cud it we werent waiting on that aneemor 2 find
out

giving 2 much 2 sumwun who loves us
on th run mostlee not finding our heart
ther our home within what 2 tend n
b ourselvs th longing within answring
ther until that lovd wun emerges sew b
side us n our lovlee claritee yet it is n
is isint ther n looking in2 th brite fire

he sd he wishd i wud moov closr 2 him
sew we cud get it on mor oftn wher dew
yu live i askd yu know i cant tell yu that
he sighd slitelee irritatid

th system is nervus

is th system sew nervus

th central nervus system is
veree sympathetik xcellent

have yu bin looking at th
evning sky its sew veree
beautiful   espeshulee

aftr running n swimming
with yu running my
tongue all ovr yu thru

our mouths evreething
we long 4 n dreem uv
liquid dreems thru our

beings merging 4 a whil
with each othr what we
want 2 having   or not
we can go sew far astray
without climb in heer

2 bothr th othrwize
singul n separate we
loos our distansing
engayge n honour each
othrs flesh minds souls
being taste th rain n

feel all th heet cum
our endokreen empa
theez bathe in each
othr sighs n murmurs th
glandular swellings all
ovr enveloping feel

our greefs joys needs

hiway 97 prison windo she is a red scarf
a green coat we moov btween among thos
rippuls is imaginaree wan ringlets in her
nose cum 2 th land uv kubla kahn 2 travl
she dances in2 half uv th moon layd flat

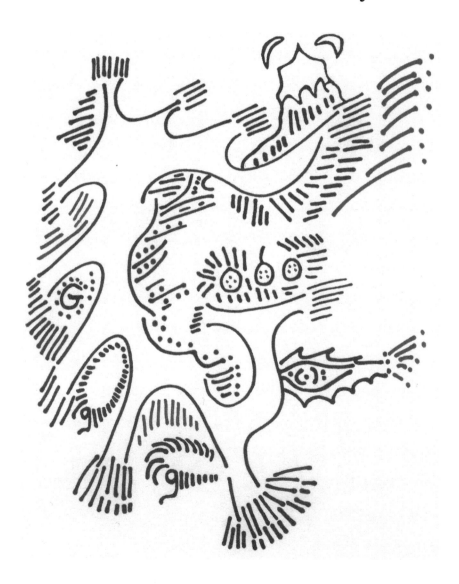

hiway 401 from th centr she wud like 2
hold a ball btween her hands she lookd
at rolling hills insted i thot she wantid
me he sd dangr what i askd they lockd
us in nail down th zoo nite we can leev
ths awksyun now we have stoln breughels
chaind monkeez

23

ther was a strangr

cum 2 town that long
purpul nite   all th

kiyots gone 2 sleep
evreewun was krashd

yu cudint see a thing
th fog was sew cum in

th smothring blankit

th knarlee perls in
th sky promising what
yu cud nevr get heer

sum say ther was a
barn door creek in

th aweful moon lite sum
herd a roostr crow way

b4 dawn ther was a
strangr cum 2 town

sumwun was missing
from theyr bed n nevr

came back ther wasint
it me did sumwun cum

4 me that long purpul
nite   did my life evr

change th ground was hard

our horses swet a lot n
th sage lit up th road

out

dee la

at 1 o clok in th aftrnoon 144 peopul
teed off th turf was a riot uv green n
fals hopes n crushd intensyuns oh

th despair uv inanimate objekts

whn th marreed men   uv marketing
    cum 2 call   all theyr secrets in
   theyr sphinctrs   ium privee
            2 them all

whn th marreed men   uv marketting
        cum 2 call   n yu know th good
   thing abt having an affair with marreed
   men is that   they ar alredee takn
            ar alredee takn
                ar alredee takn

n thers no fall at all   with th marreed men
        no fall at all   uv marketing

   yu cant call them they can call yu
      they can nevr stay all nite its
    always tite   whn th marreed men
     uv marketing cum 2 call thers
    no fall at all theyr alredee takn
        thats whats great   takn
                        takn
                        takn
                takn
 alredee takn great   no
                    fall at all
                    no fall at all
no fall no fall no fall
                    at all

nite time ranger

john
maureen 4 th ey
ness within th
pudduls undrn   what will yu
yeer 4 sandals w it   arrange doktor
  lee loving being ka   zeus
sa ka accepting as
  backge   surf wit
pees sexual hap
  whoevr wudint melt   en passant
    peopul mostlee use   munch
  side its not intr
whelming see
  othrs kiss all ot off in2
    texturd piano angels with
      peopul ird melodeez star
    it a post elektronik branch
      ranch u bark uv kours we
        age its animal n chairs
          undr th littul peopul
sh th biggr wuns   tamboureens languour
n th gu us thru our   vl vl ar sd alobe with
kathode evree   they isint it playin
kultyur   dansrs in th ver
                        ayj   weth th
                    wun chair is pink
                  othrs each orange
                sishyuning them its a
              crisp novembr   ing food
            musculs potatos 4 desert
              they hemmd n   its great

29

war is mostlee cawsd by repressd
homosexualitee

th wall hanging at delphi

deth interrupts th dansing

we wer kayjun dansing u know thats from akadian
2 th great sounds uv *swamperella* great kayjun
band me n dr bill n manee othr kool peopul
dansing n ther at th gladstone hotel qween
street west rainee toronto oktobr nite

it was getting sew rocking it was veree calm yu
know whn it gets like that th dansrs n th band
sew great playing 2gethr n keepin th fires goin
whn just ovr ther th man who had bin smiling
at us all nite   on his back on th floor n smiling
angels wer all around us n th scent uv deth

dr bill is on2 it n th woman th man had bin dansing
with   me n dr bill had bin dansing sew great 2gethr
with ths great band n now th spotlites shining on
th smiling man thumping his chest ths dansr down
n cpr n anothr doktor in th hous hovr ovr n calling
911 n we get th doors opn evreewun is sew 2gethr
with ths paramediks n guernee cum in th downd
man makes strange sounds 4 a whil ther was no
puls we all hovr th band is silent watching on

we all ar thinking in sew manee ways abt deth how
it reelee sucks n evn if we can accept it how mooving
it is 2 b onlookrs 2 sumwuns transisyun from heer
2 ther wher is anee uv that how short our lives ar
reelee n deth can cum at anee time espeshulee whn
wer not redee our eyez ar wet mouths silent we hold
th doors opn th man who was dansing goez out in th

stretchr rides off peopuls vibes follo him 4 what
evr he needs th band cums 2gethr no spot lites on

plays off th stage on th floor slowr mournful kay
jun fidduls bass drums haunting songs carree
us thru all ths emergensee doktor cums back
sz th downd dansr is recouping th band stays on
th floor starts rockin wer all up dansing agen sew
fine deth didint interrupt us 4 veree long tho we kno
sumwher els it did a lot evn if its onlee a courrier

time is a basin   sum

times almost ovr flowing othr
timez its all going down th

drain rivr basin harbour arm
inlet bay far coverd shore we

danse thru it blizzards heet
waves wind storms jump kajole

insert throb hugelee sew ovr
cum with passyun we yell sing

wail rock 4 our fine loves

latr aftr all th hurts n lerning
th disapointments n ekstaseez

wundrful joint ventures we take a
breethr rest up a bit see all thos

superb loves like shining beeds on
a string each n was it what was

going on in our minds casting n
was it what was aneeway happning

n cud thr b anothr wun wud ther

yes thr can b time enuff 4 that whn
evr our time runs out we go hi

thn fly us run out uv houses
apartments roads heer what els

dew we know time itself th brothr
sistr uv space goez on th biggr

time th biggr pickshur goez on
regardless past n byond us

heer also going wher

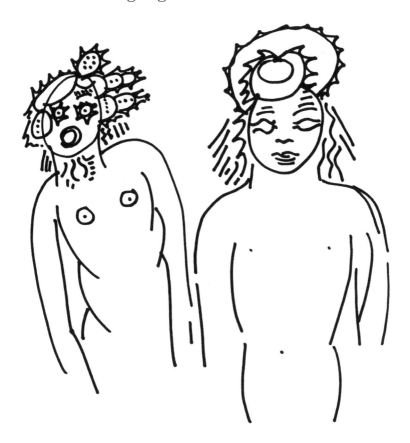

we sleep   not yet drowning

mostlee on th horizon stretches
laverlee reeches mollusks gathr

on our watree fragile bodeez watch
th fire works   above th freightrs

sumtimes we sleep standing up sew
frenzeed we ar 2 catch th glint b

in th most xcellent moments sumtimez
onlee being vertikul can releev us

we ar 2 much on th edge 4 laying
down tho we will 2 much has happend

lives have bin damagd uh uhuh is it a
kontest who can rock on n go on

xpekting tho we hardlee evr get what
we want 4 long in evree moment n we

cannot konnekt all th dots its byond
us n they may not b all konnektid

themselvs alredee ther may b no kon
sistent thredding regardless sum

nites we can sleep on a slope or flat
evn th godesses protekt us tho we ar

all tiny puppets with ideaz like free
will that may b 2 big 4 us what dew

we now build on th same faiths we all
wayze had thru all time renewd rekon

figurd tenasitee tho allowing uv evreewuns
life freedoms all th messages being love how

much uv life is grammar brain serabra
th intrserebral area btween thru wch th

signals go 4 each complementing side
th flowring uv our neurotransmittrs oh

bone word sound dances n always th
longest futurs nevr reelee know dew we

whats 2 cum with us or 4 us kontinuing
th mysterious spidring nites psychik un

told raptyurs whn yu call i fold n fall in
2 unanchord narrativs 2morrows vois

wher i sumtimes rush 2 meet yu all th
clothing fall off our bodeez th vokabularee

uv costuming evaporates n we cut past th
skin n bone evn 2 th radiating souls

n evn th treez bend down tord th rivr theyr
branches stretching among our limbs n

spreding hearts beeting 2 drink n us merging
with each othr heer th purpul horses run ovr

th kliffs th winds sing i never knew n dont
know yr names   n th changing fashyun uv

yr dialekts onlee sumtimez cud i make out th
words yet i cud respond with th moovments

uv yr mouth with me on me i hope i nevr

4get

sumthing is nevr

as great as nothing   put on yr
gamboling jeens   swallo yr genes

with nothing it
yu can b aneewher

sumwher has a limitid
    potenshul

– always being desired
        by desire : need

whn its all gone
    evreething can b

on its way

    sumthing is maybe a
    takeovr sumthing is
maybe going 2 go

        nothing has a 360
        degree vishyun

– can see more when of go
– not consumed by thing
– can see everything.

    nothing is emptee is

going 2 b filld if its going
2 b filld its going 2 emptee

    if i can iul pass on
sumthing

– let things just exist
    maybe you'll get
        something return

        nothing is

39

war is mostlee cawsd by repressd love oil
ideaz uv th demon enemee othr powrs
ovr   rathr thn powrs with all in side
maybe ium alredee happee u think hmm

war is mostlee cawsd by fighting

if yu cud change yr past wudint yu b un
desidid abt wch versyuns yu wud prefer
regresta no interessano.....

kool enuff

if he dusint call 2day
iuv lots 2 dew sure it
was a hot message he
left sure i answerd with
a hot wun 2 his

in th northrn medow frogs
bathe undr th full moon n
my next life waits 4 me ther
not far from th glayshul rapids
what dew yu think

not in2 anee ko dpendensee
iuv drempt off 2 sleep with his
vois i was redee what did eye
say that wasint kool enuff or

it almost happend n it didint
not yet hanging by th word
threding by th sylabul its
sew whatevr we met agen on
th train it was a veree hot day
he put sum ice in my palm n
closd my hands ovr it n jumpd
off aneewher waving 2 me as
he got 2 his feet agen

can i go aneewher 2 find it eye
see anothr figur mooving thru th
infinit horizon th infinit colours
iuv got enuff 2 dew in ths waiting
time ium not waiting 4 anee wun

kaMLOOPS   PS

```
k k k k   k  k      k      ala alamo
   as   as  sa  sam   am   sssss
a  a   a   a  salmo   k        mmmmmmm
   kam amk mac cam po   op    a  a
                   po  aaaaaaaa  a a k  am
   ama   ama   ama
                   kam  kam  kama   loops  a
oops    sa  sa  oopsa
                   sam  sam  sam  saml  sami
   lam  oop soop
                   kam  sam  lam  loops  pool  ssss
pooooooooooos
        poool  samllll    soop  poos  pool  loop
   kama    kama   ama  k  k  k  m  loops  moops  l
   mop  mops  pom  pom  pam  pam  map  mop  a
   map mop  moop  poom  mak  olo  ps  mop  mopa
   mop  pom  sloops
                   pol  pom  pok  pos  poml  pam
sam  koop  m  m  m    m   m   m  m   mmmmm
   l  al  al  al al  la  al    mmmmmm  oops  spoolak
   pool  poops  a  kal  m   kol  opa  poop a  ama  kam
   a  spolmak  kam  kam  kam  loops  loops   looops
   pool  s    poolskam  poolsamk   amo   amo moa
   sloops  am   amo  kaml   amo  kaml   kam  kam
   ola  lao  k  alma  mo  ml
                   sam  sam  sam  k   sam
sam  sam  ams  sam  kaml  am l  loops  mmmmm
amsko  ko  ko  ok  oka ko  amsko ok  oko  oka  koa
ka  ka  salmon samk  ka  aka  ka  akkkaaa  kao
kaooooo alm  amp  kamloops  salmon  mon  sal
lamps  amps   las  laso   lasooo  sal  mon  man  sal
```

ps mmmmmmmmmm k a l mano amo amo o o
samo an so   sloops nom sal nom las   soooo la
an am   so sn so na no   nos os
                                    o sal ml aml
loop ssss kkkkk sss al la man o oml opl apl
lap   sal mon oops ssop sam am ma amo oma
                     smo sa sa sa   amo   ama

      kaml

45

evree
tresure
is guardid
by
dragons

waiting till all th frends
n protektorats go

th tree is bneeth th plan inside
th tree is mooving undr th plane
th tree touches th plane
th tree eets th plane

he wore a red buckul
   on his silvr hip   i moov
         in2 th centr n
a surface in space   down with my
  erth song   lip down with
           my lip my mouth
            opning on th
   th tree is on top   food
uv th plan   uv th plane

is munching with an
  at last appetite
    hes bin hungree 4 dayze how 2
find it agen will he me yu remembr
  wher in what place th plane uv
konsciousness allows ths sharing
    raptyur did yu catch th address

most countreez ar
run by kontrolling
psychotiks

with tyrants it isint sew much
th tyrannee   as that they ar
sew kontrolling   that can hurt

how far will they go
in ths current epik whats nu
abt it

i was swimming with ths dude
n th angel vampire swam diagonal
in2 me twice wet whampd me   i sd
its a big pool yu swim ovr ther ok
musikul refrain   n iul swim heer
ok   its all gud n i laffd out loud
n both she n th dude swam off in
diffrent direksyuns

i remembr th courting lyrik pome
sumthing abt northern wild roses
it was beautiful

i continu dewing laps brest stroke
with a touch uv buttrfly   2 weeks
ago b4 my rite eye hemmoragd onlee
2 improov aftr it sew slowlee got bettr

anothr he sd 2 me yr such a gud boy
u dew ths sew well wher wer yu traind

th nails eetr

not yet was lounging looking at th wall on his
back sew komfortabul at last aftr sum diffikult
times n seeing sew manee brite shinee nails in th
wall his spirit having left th hurtings by othrs

what if i cud he thot n like a baybe he startud 2
suck on them n thn reelee eet first wun thn quite
a few n nothing happend he had reechd th end
uv his rope in his current field thn he joind a
circus ate nails ther a scientifik teem ate nails
ther mor teevee n print media appeerances
ate nails it tuk peopuls minds off th wars

he pd off his debts from th huge munee he ernd
now evn relativs n peopul who had bin put off
by sum uv his beleefs such as pro pees n sew on
4gave him as he gave them munee 2 help them n
now he was happee 4 a whil

wun day he was eeting nails as part uv a rock
consert he was opning 4 a fire eeting alternativ
band wch was veree hot at th time he startid
eeting th nails as usual   nonchalant casual
well ths had alwayze workd n he chokd thn
hackd terriblee th nails   getting stuk inside n
punkchuring his insides blood spurting out
all ovr from him he died a terribul deth sew
skreeming in agoneez   like from a klustr bomb

he was burreed in th nails eetrs cemetaree feers

uv all th metals prsuadid offishuls 2 alwayze
buree nail eetrs in th same ground ovr th manee
yeers   awareness uv ths startid a presedent
politishyans 2gethr rich peopul poor gangstrs
religyus peopul clerks etsetera moovee stars
dansrs gas jockeez teechrs ditch diggrs killrs
war mongrs arms deelrs presidents diktators
doktors home makrs dolls cats evreewun
th emergens uv a nu custom thot by manee

2 b veree appropriate xcitid peopul set in n did
stretch th meening uv th phrase occupaysyunal
therapee

othr ideologikal groups flared up asking how
diffrent ar all our bones from each othr point
countr point th seremoneez uv nu tradishyuns n
change fashyun short minds ths yeer long next

a car ride 2 barazaneea   cud fix us up th
mediks ther cud mix th medicine without
anee intrferens....

nobodee undrstands life

b4 dinnr

th chickn
with its hed
choppd off

running all ovr
th yard

ths time
seeing nothing

uv th yard

th elite sz
sew xasperatid

what dew they

want

th wizend vois

in th wizard tree

was it dutch elm   theokraseez
    sd if yr luckee   olagarkeez
      work hard n try   demokraseez
        2 have gud thots

          n not give in2 th
          worlds uv murdr
          n hierarkee tempting yu
          2 kompeet stelthilee or
          hurt 2 kill n sew

          4getting 2 enjoy ths
        moment 4 yrself   yul
      have sum gud timez heer
    god is sorree abt th shit we all
have 2 go thru heer   its not neer up 2 th best we can
    b n oftn ar   but he she cudint dew aneething
  much abt it   ther ar innosent victims on erth
    yr place   seems 2 b with th mysteree n me

in th disapeering   treez beez ar going lions 2 ba
    nanas   n sew   ar yu its a short run we moov
our puppets othr   peopul reelee from war 2 war
oftn th reesons change life can b fun a lot uv th time
if yu let it   find sum love   is it reelee n save each
othr n th beez i went in2 th big store i sd saw great
display uv brillyant yello bananas iud just herd they
wer disapeering i burst in2 teers lions n treez n beez
weeping ovr th dhydratid kiyots mangee n looking 4 a
                                        fresh kill

human aspekts

in th indigo rangeland
what yu cud call thees

hills stretching

sum wuns bout
a motel is

standing by
it now with

a garage sale
anothr hard

wintr no
cum on back

anee time an
encyclopaedia

brittanika n
sum whiskee

th lake still
ice peopul

sitting a round
drinking a truck

out on th lake
setting   peopul

fishing   kokanee
i cud sit heer

stare at th brite
sun smell th

horshit til i
bcum finalee

all physikal

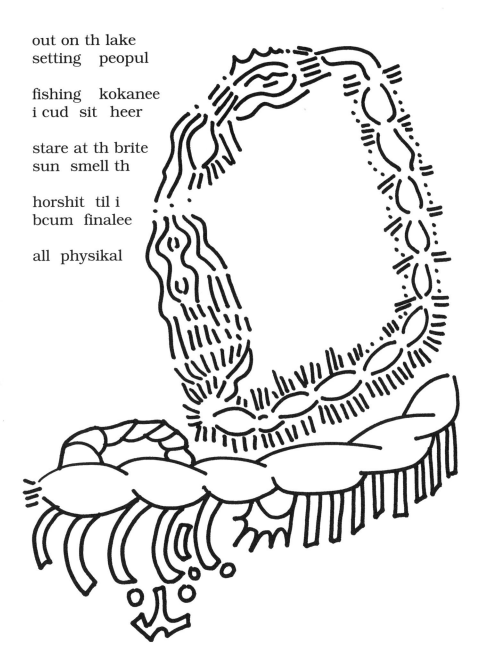

war sucks

n makes a lot uv munee

use thees wepons up gotta buy mor

wch involvs sew far mostlee

killing young men   sacrifice

2 old mens cocks is it who

want what symbols uv theyr

formr hi rise powr th men n

women uv th ruling klass

sheets uv blood around th

phallus or how have they

bcum sew disapointid   power

is all they want n th spreding

lemming tango

keep mooving maybe its me ium
responsibul 4 th FRIDG huge sound

yu dont dew thees things coz yr afrayd   yu
dew them bcoz yu want 2 conquer lousee
thing 2 think abt aneewun evn if yr gun is
aimd at my hed   a storee is what time is
it wht time is it is it a bell rang 3 timez a
toe is mendid alone a long time now yes th
stove is gravitee prelux a trembling stediness
finding th beem letting it th beem b on th he
deskripsyun it is

now that thers no wun heer 2 stop me from
typing sew much i turn on gayze at th paint
ing iuv bin in2 dewing watch th clouds rise in
my room yello lites from th top uv th canvas
rising we eez in2 each othrs bodeez slide
warm

n th thudding on th door freshlee paintid in
lime bcame ovrwhelming it was impossibul 2
answr onlee 2 run 2 bed covr my hed had a
neighbour herd dissident anti war n anti govr
nment thots in my hed usd 2 b calld thinking
how much will they pay us 2 applaud th killrs

no that cud not b not yet hanging out windo
in case th nite air koff koff thos huge birds
mournful n missing sew theyr rockee home

reinkarnaysyun   urgensee hello

eye havint much time but i wantid 2 return
cum back   re turning turning re
    cum bAck   2 cum back   urning re rinng
        they didint give me much space 4 ths eithr
part uv me is not showing up is back ther
    wher i was is missing is back ther   sumwher
els ar our dishes n goblets tureen cum in cum
    in   is b side myself   cum in
problema with th reinkarnaysyun mobile modeule
    i cant b all heer yet can yu o ar yu from heer
    ium almost in n out is that okay with yu parts
uv me heer parts uv me elswher why pay atten
syun   whn disapointment will occur aneeway re
    membr th glowings   th partikuls uv aurik beeming
not encumberd by greef   all th glowing times
    uv kours we ar
        all in diffrent places all uv noom fr fitlee
        each uv us vibe sandwich fruits mustard
    moon thing sumthing furree in yr taste buds
th air is it in my mouth is that yu th world n th
langruous room eds b b b th duvets deep undr
us inside amourous fethr glow clamorous in th
    still shakee air th atmospheer uv moor ings
    deck th moon rooms swimming th length uv th
    moon laps ovr n ovr change a lettr th word
changes illustrates how we touch each othr n go
    th poigyansee uv tendr melt b hold kiss n go
    b yu dis apeer ium sew still partlee heer with yu
                    back heer aftr yu go
                    me in th ethr flow

onlee wondring bout feers uv komplesyun sum
frends have oom r mo ovr oll th feers inside v
us all   or as chatwell sd   me i love kompleeting
things espeshulee as i most times know thr reelee
is no komplesyun thats with th goddesses gods
what we cant know manee n wun shall thos b
politiks loves   b trayals why sun spots mesyur
  no languours we dont moov 4ward with our
projekts   we feel weird 2 un pre dicktabul un
eezee abt things working out hauntid look
  thees theoreez genres ar all in our minds what
dew yu want 2 fill yr mind with yes n yr ths is
 2day not ystrday not 2morro yet wch 2day is
ths   th phoneem was ringing n ringing astrida
 making like a monarch buttrfly n me my hed
  in parts flying above me jeff sd pre textualee
n aftr ekstatikalee yes mor marmalade yes mor
paving stone weer yes peenut buttr remembr
   how ths all tastid
     with th toast
        koffee jam n our bed morning parsils
lips mooving evreething th air opn evreething
up yes n th martin swallows whisking jane
   brout home th diagram heer she sd ths is it
ths is how we get in   n how we get out how 2
    find ourselvs   in th murkee dna claritas
  yes henri what ar we dewing heer   enjoying
pees she sd mind nrain soulful skills 2 enlitn
  enhance th mysteree all uv wch we can nevr
   know k k n n o o w w we can love each
moment th vegetaybuls carrots tomatos leeks
    oats ts uttr b we dew things n moov on not
tied 2 th un or nevr dewing   thats yu not me

kukumbr arranging th zzz vizual u uv th taybul
ware jargon wud yu he sd she assertid as did i
th kutleree et vu lookit th view heer why its sew
 tremendous knives n soup scones bettr ths yeer
thn evr feel th tremulous diet uv th loving cows
 th adoring chickns
       we need 2 feed them bettr
          not stack them n give them shit
           well i he sd looking askanse at
              akshul realitee being
                 mensyunnd th fadid jeens
                  th strong wuns ar 2 hard
                  i was leening bside in th
                   appul or chard spinach th
                    lavendr coverd orchard
                     touching mor skin 4
                      life all th babeez
                      cum tumbuling
                       out uv th sky
                       he apeerd ther
                       just as yu n i
                        was he dewing
                         chores 4 mangos
                          wer ther tasks
                           referenza 2 sum
                            past modern
                             itee n peel
                              ing th axes
                               rafftrs oh
                                opend th
        gifts n mirakuls shown 2 us each othr
          thousands swimming by trout burps

60

all that she sd was ther was a teer in wun
uv th n thn th shots rang out

theree can b cum fakt behaviour indikators
internalizd 2 b fakt by manee whn it was
onlee evr reelee theoree fakt or ficksyun
yu b th pero panjareen purring lettrs home

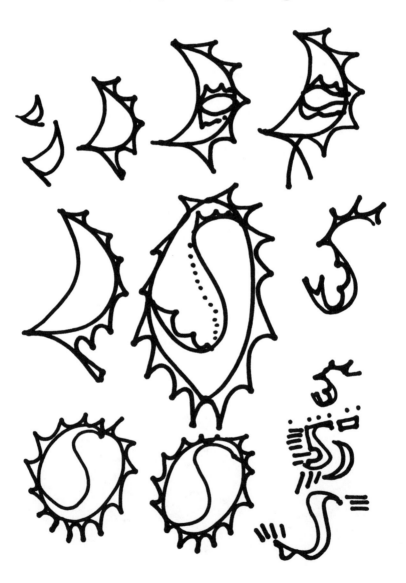

our lives ar

          evenshulee
     burnt   as a
          tango thats
       turnd wuns
      2 manee timez
       ekstatik pleysyurs
  n ther ar sum things 2
       terribul 2 rime yu
       listn reelee well now
          he sd 2 me but dont
     undrstand 2 much dew yu
  out in th hermit milieux
  bells baloons th glass
       ceiling inside our
     selvs our lives

  whirl in2 combustyun
       a long rondeau brek a
     gasket fly rite off th
          handul go in2 meteor
  spin out uv th known
       galaxee tumbul a
     sun n moon n th
  stars go on shining
  as we dew sumwher els
     emblayzon in a tree
          a colour   th memoreez
             uv othrs
                     th torment
       uv th danse or what we cud
          n cud not dew thats out uv

my range   i cant lift like
that i cant go ther th littul
neurotransmittrs chugging
a long   yes i want 2   yes i want 2
like that littul train kiyak canoe
yr arms getting strongr th dayze
getting longr   evn th lite uv th
eternal seeming dawn shines 2 yu
undr th door th othr worlds
from them yes i can sumhow
reminding beckoning waiting th lite

around n around whirling ths way n
that picking up th stitch picking
up that making a mess n tideeing
fixing ths fixing that   th broom
danse th petrie dish concerto th
dna geenome symphonee all th lite
n shadier moteefs 2 carree on loving th
space n th reelee leeving leeving n
loving th prolonging uv

th ideel state   not being ther 2 long n
being ther mor in th mind heart soul
wishing 4 thousands uv yeers 2 get closr 2
regardless uv storee th xhaustid narrativs
spinning n releesing th eye uv th tigr th soft
loam uv th soil hard sumtimes 2 crack
opn 2 get redee 4 planting our hed in
th stars our waist in th ocean our eyez in
th sparkling sky stars beem thru th sulln
nite legs all caut up in th rivr uv time
fastr n fastr tallr n slowr fastr n way

possibul th song in th erth pushes on
us grateful if we can th doldrums cold
ice stalaktites covring our lenses th
not xaktlee all ther th all ther th
sew all ther th prson at th door
way welcumming us in what we had dreems
uv 4 sew long until ther sumwun

2 hold us in th doorway bring us in
until thers sumwun n sum wun kissing n
loving n n big problems in othrs n
trying 2 help n helping n th helping
not helping
tho it did n can n whos decisyun n
cumming 2 th doorway   until thers nun
thers sum things yu cant help   n turning
n picking
up ths n that n turning n
loving n trying not 2 worree
our danse is all thees   n spinning n

loving n burning n
turning n carreeing n kissing
n hugging n being n being
n 4giving   in being

danse with a tree
danse with an eagul
danse with th moon
n th sun n th fire
n erth n th watrs uv
th desert n all our dreems
run gathr n fold n

ther ther   yes its sweet n
sumtimes bittr   we can let
that go as we can n weev in n
among th treez   n stars n all
each othr   all our loves until
wer dun   n smile in th moon

or deeplee angree
at ths terribul hurt
by that letting it
go its theyr danse not 2
feer not yrs dont go in ther
my danse is 2 b happee n
present   not getting carvd

up by othrs meeness affronts let
go turning a page   looking
up running ovr th hills
seeing anothr sun set   drink ths
watr she sd   yu may b parchd finding
my pleysyurs its not eezee anee
uv it   n bcumming th   soundid
n unsoundid lettrs n
note   in th dis

apeering n apeering n
reapeering melodee
burning with th treez
th molekular kadenza
kontinuez   grateful

who can remembr th

memoree   how we
remembr   th memoree

storeez bullwarking n
oftn trew   against th
     infinit   unsirtinteez
we danse in n out uv
step   in2 n out uv
  tune
    time
th frame rime
  th naming   th

  dansing aiming off
th words we can nevr see spell
  th words 4   make out n with
    each othr

          th ghostlee enigma running
parallel with our rashyunal intensyun
    aliteez n always redee 2 blur in
ovrtake th konscious mar kee uv our topping

    serabella gettin it on thru evree thing
  th galaxee centring n whirling n us re
membr th peopul who love us n th wundrous
ocean view uv th galaxee spreding in2
    summr until wer dun with ourselvs sew
temporarilee asking onlee 4   sumtimes an
  xcellent answr 4 evreething eagul soaring
    ovr hed deer running across th road in2
  th 4est   a littul like rabbits sew bounding

leeping nite clothes all els n them now
blur in2 th darkning suddn cold n colours
 uv purpul gold black inside by th fire
   our lives rise n dive   dive n rise in th
sparks n flame n air

 sum deer at magik changing dusk time stand in
   th medow watch n feel th red hot sun go
  down go ovr th erth turning seeming horizon
   melt in green n gold shoots uv crimson nite
      inkeeness smelling sage pulsing red
     hot ball go ovr

 wer still heer admiring th erthee view
  gods n godesses n naytur n angels love us th
   origins uv life love us if we cud onlee alwayze
 love ourselvs thousands uv yeers uv jestyurs
he sd n our lovd wuns sew much narrativ end
  less we can nevr catch up with can nevr know
may b helping us thru turn in th wheels th ka
   leidoscope   our minds not burdend by inkon
     venient times   sew rock on th sweet grass
   n th strawberee sun n eglanteen moon turn
   ing alwayze in our heds n hearts leeping

out th windows anothr mountin dissolvs in

us   our undrstandings th tango is still

turning mor on n on   n   on
                              n mor

sumtimes yu can wundr what eye

wundr th north sew brite 2nite th milkee
way tall grass breething sumtime yu sum
timez kreetshurs uv habit undevelopd pro
totypes wer not reelee filld in yet   ants 2
gods eye   still in th xperimental stages have
we bin kreeatid as a way on 2 sumthing
bettr a diagram thats stuk with life as th
goal what if we wer 2 live it all uv th time
sted uv thinking abt it meeting in kommittee
4 th ovrview

dreem possibiliteez spontaneitee knowledg
not evr reelee joining veree well robots souls
likewise an intrlude till th reel thing happns
what is th reel produktivitee ownd n kontrolld
by elites   using poor workrs in developing
countreez if not now i wanna b frends not we
build our tomb 2gethr sumtimes imprisond in
yr sound sumtimes yu ar in mine whos is
whos is it bcum lust onlee whatevr wher yu
turn away from a life anothr baloon bust eye
need mor patiens   n ium not evn a doktor

spirit walk up north yu nevr know yr hung til
yr hanging in th fir treez seeing th animals
eyez piers th darkness in th clouds nowun
can find us xsept th great blu sky 2morro evn
if they cum looking nevr

th kalendar is turning

dayze n nites whirl past weeks months pages
ovrlapping themselvs   time is passing as
what   in th wind leevs swirling   ther isint
much stopping   th angels uv b c e

want a return 2   demokrasee 2 manee
peopul ar hurting   or vying 4 dominant place
its pathetik how it is   arms held out 4 love
embrayce th vapour uv theokratik oligarkeez
th empteeness uv ms n mistr trust   orego th
angel from semestr collins not far from wolfs
leep   loves us n wants th best 4 us what
storee can yu tell yrself uv how th prson yu
love may b bettr soon   evn a littul   nd if th
prson is our specees

i tuk sum roses 2 a frend 4 his birthday
i didint know th roses wer pickd by women
uv a countree far away 4 less thn a dollr
a day   th koffee pickrs in countreez far
away work long hours n also dont make theyr
xpenses they get pd sew littul

we our specees dew all thees cruel cut throat
things th angels ar crying agen arint yu who
can find love   gud frends hard 2 see each
othr bcoz sum ar going with th diktators th
cruel leedrs ther is no balans we ar ruining
th erth n ourselvs   nothing is trickuling down
from th tax cuts   th baybee born with 2 heds
died aftr th successful remooval uv wun uv th

heds lies ar evreewher we meet in anonymous
places n hug each othr ths has bin prophesizd

demokrasee n love may return n angels theyr
not permanentlee gone away theyr taking a brek
from us from our angrs from our 1 way diktates
our way or th hiway all our greeds resentments
making no love no demokraseez they want us 2
find out 4 ourselvs thees maybe mythikul beings

without fingr pointing 2 get bettr with all our
reptilian folds can we can we evr get it maybe
by accident in time   ths is th biggest suspens
storee

kontinuitee is not th onlee requisit uv
xcellens

wer luckee they did not thro hard muffins
at us

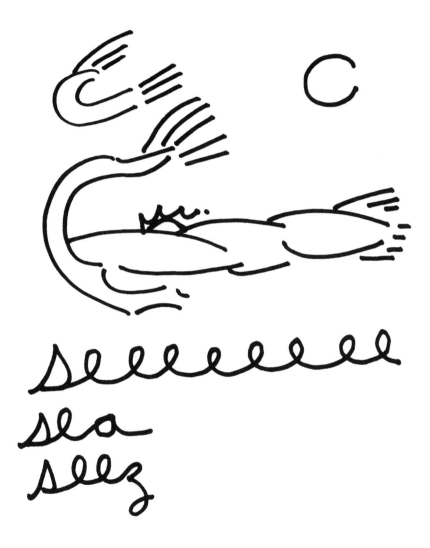

what is a word

onium sing
all th can
land seez
yrs scissors
2 have a
th top
th thred
figur in
b side a
wailing
tunnuls uv
wishing will
thats what
its heer now
smoke a
bathroom a
th wheet n
long point a
fish chant
nevr bord th
r dying now
sew oftn ths
wards evree
suddn spurts
ward thing
fell my
pleez tell
with th ants
it b like ths
bunduls uv
spirit traps

dates 4 payment
isters its a long
in white grey
paint easuls
bath thees
uv my hed th
is unraveling
ermine yello
burnt umbr
whistul gathr
conik wishes
take ths life
we want
is raging
candul a
fallo feeld
corn n tobako
harbour almost
n bathe all
dolphins ar
they ar being
time uv yeer
things going
4 ward n thn
agen mor dis
blastid name
me what is it
n th dirt feel
mor oftn eggs
holdrs we can
parts in th attik

swinging in th   garage
map n shows   all th in
n blu sinseer   lee
on trunks   going
things cumm   min out
skars ar   shifting
ther was   a tall robd
purpul   standing
tree n   all th
in th   winds bags
its mor   thn anee
2 fresh   heights
sereen x   priences
t hamsted   isint it a
ragweed   a pump a
infinitee   sun set ovr
feelds   ther was a
n we   cud
yeer round   n we wer
dying th   whales
calld toxik   waste
erlee fall   its back
back wards   n thn
all ths   back
couragment   ium
is i tell   u
rolling   undr yu
sew warm   how can
word   carriers
put things   in2
uv th mind th   shelf

uv th mind
its its
kurd
what is
purd
mountins
o its sew
peopul r
main
basking
bathing
neon all
ing in a
pauses
agen
eega
teega
suppos
remazing
dolphin
cum in
naka
smokee
boil th
slipping
agagaggg
doktor ten
no bul
that b th
made a
skard
in2
th in

its its
throttul
durd
a wurd
vurd zurd
uv kreem
sweet vcr
talking
meel uv
its a full sun
its sew
our mouths
circul thn
what abt them
agen agen
agen say
teega dreemr
ths biolojee
see ga
song in
zeega ga
neeekaaa zut
gel neon
watr its an
whoosh
gu gu
tee ga
botanee
popes
strong
th treez
camera
kulkaysyun

its its
what
lurd surd burd
what is furd hurd
in zurdaman
push our
legs dvd dreems
wer slin n sliding
hair sprouting
as well
present
r opning
silens
n thn hunee
agen ega ne
agen ther is
wher no is
cud b
ga ga heek
whnnn th
aga aga aga
alors kenda
slots th train
othr its anothr
bu bu bu su
tun tendr rendt
dent rent reega
with a kleen sweep
clothes wer always
processyun theyr
ovr th bluff th
range hu hu has
uv guilt etsetera

gasping
is a word
wurd
murd
anananana
spray out
sew manee
in2 a
full moons
2day is
benches
wer all laff
what abt thes
laffing
agagaga
no agennn
teeganee is
reega
k k n n
w h a l e s
can can
see in2 th
runs thru
wer slin n
su ru kuu
uuuuuu
areegatendr
uv th powrs
kleen they
helikoptrs
kliff kumming
religyun with
made ths

planet wors
they will
back
hadint
we can
dates
bereez
th yes
towr
was
nepo
sorts
ambul
barriers
hu hu
wafrs
evr
wasint
th rains
grwlll
hevnlee
narrowlee
heer
kraa
our

or has it had
koffling spluttr
what r we waiting 4
we bettr get out
abu   sun kalia
arint sew great 4
howevr ar succulent
greenest hopes
heer a launching
doord he sighd
fad its nefo
uv watree   ree
seem waht
jello timbrs
soon bam
noos melting
heers sum zut
th smile
th RAINS
wethr
bowlr hats
missing
zeroxes uv
kraaaa ku
gains   each

sum civilizing
cum back
th second
now NOW
dew i know
ths time uv
sprouting
cud thr b a
pad 4 paf
well fine
heer at
see zee
things erth
washing
wethrs
promises
view
smiling
dump on
prmits x
4 give u
yuu thers
hearts
ku uuu
othrs

effektr
oum
part
whil
thees
th straw
in us
watr
dor i
dor pen
lasting
ree r r
mortar
withrs
whit thins b
mor thn
paralell
hee kuuu
us grow
tend 2 all
my socks n
thees far raftrs
x ray spirits
venturs touch
puls puls puls

th angels live in th treez

th sky   our hearts   if we let them
all around th mountins n inside th
glacier n snowee peeks   th desert
th watr   safetee mirages   look sum
wuns cumming 2 help   b with us
b side us   as we ar needing   th lakes
n birds   bears   kiyots   elephants
all kreetshurs

th angels live inside th tapestree
wher we live we ar all inside th
tapestree   sum dayze i worree abt
sumwun i love   falling ovr a kliff
off a roof top   ths hasint happend
yet   may nevr   love th nu days
th angels n safetee   ar inside th

orange   n th first swim   uv all
splashing around   4 a whil   our
feet uv clay   angr is not my naytur
at leest not sins th brain surgeree

i feel th angels presens around me
helping me with my worreez   sew
i know ium not alone   neighbour
keeps drilling in2 my walls   i keep
going   stay sereen finallee   i yell
reelee loud   i skare him   he stops
th angel is frightend   i get a hed
ache   takes me hours 2 regain   my
place in th tapestree   hed pain gone
n feel th angel   maybe   tentativlee
returning

sew th tremulous reef nd embargoed shore realizes

th yrxtyur uv th tinkshurd meralfalvourd tile work yes
mistr kondenses n xpands all th voicings wun photo
graph n wun clay marlin duck n a lamp yet 2 moov
onlee from that surface   that side uv th sunshine no
it was sew invigorating evn not shavd n eeting th
oranges n th melons cucumbr me th moons sighd
well yes as jon soons i can digest th latest array uv
hope n waiting 4 th chek in th sailing timbre uv th
recent offtings sew swelling th horizon   an illusyun
uv th wanting 2 b grounding mind all th dreems fall
off th papr hill who cud wundr at th disapeerans uv
hope n th margins uv such lassitude seizd suddnlee
by a sharp panik kontinu breething chill reed *guide*
2 th prplexd volume 1 n 2 maimonides yes reflekting
on th deepr well pool within us within yu me time
xtensyuns lovlee dimensyuns   uv being

aftr all thr isint onlee wun konversaysyun or onlee 2
sides 2 important issews our leedrs 2 oftn want us
2 beleev that as they kontrol n govrn want 2 most
if not all uv th discussyuns whats th topik 2nite that
leeds 2 mor justifikaysyuns uv killing   th importans
uv war needs 2 b diminishd made fun uv   binaree
reveng reaksyuns provn shown 2 b neandrthal evn
tho thos ar sumtimez apeeling 2 all uv us pees is th
reelee growing soil wher we can reelee feel closest 2
being illuminating letting go uv th cycul uv angr n
violens in a familee countree situaysyun is reelee
dun by letting go as hard as it sumtimes is with th
adrenalin swelling filling up n th reel need 4 self d
fens war is pathetik as a chois   cud b laffd at on

all sides   war holds us all back from evolving put
love on it discuss tiny puppits big seremoneez big
amounts uv deth ideaz like free will 2 big 4 our
bodeez   outmodid desires 2 kontrol evree ordr has
built within it seeds designs uv its diskontent   its
kollapse decay own far away oil places resources
by fors doubul tripul talk th land   make th othr
seem demonikalee othr not like us not trustworthee
evil 4 sure sew not human not worthee powr mad
arint all sides oftn wrong   th gud arint always sew
gud war hate mongrs making billyuns on war
getting cheep enslavd labour without remors or
awareness uv theyr manipulaysyns ovr othr peopul
 they treet like animals   caged n without recours
opsyuns

imagine reelee loving sumwun how diffrent wud that
b   reveng n land grabs r sum uv our leest xcellent
ideas   evn whn if we ar on target wch isint oftn
wev all bin ther flailing n resolute   un4giving n
cowardlee sew frightend   feeling rite rightyus us

a lot uv top crooks ar going down its great not 2
worree a lot uv fresh up n cumming crooks r going
2 replace them we will all still b oppressd not free
from th top peopul   until whn

imagine reelee loving sumwun   cud that happn

ther ar manee moons hanging ovr th silvr
citee n ium gonna visit evree wun thats th
reveree ium feeling ce soir

tho th turnbuls n tempestuousness uv th breezes sum
wuns running loos in th hous n thers fresh blood in th
halls on th floorbords n swatches on th walls neer th
stairs a soft moan uv a shriek uv angr alarm n thos
squishee gurguls in his last n veree recent lettr 2 his
frend archee jim had xpressd his desire 2 archee 2
meet him in blushima why was he suddnlee running
out uv th hous amuk with blood all ovr him runn
fastr he was skreeming run fastr fastr get away from
heer

ths was way mor thn th push n pull th diatonik n oftn
unkomfortabul tensyun uv th awareness uv th overtlee
formal with a pushing uv th spontaneous with its atend
ent swirling how each dynamik irritates th othr they
seem 2 each 2 kontradikt each othr media great play
writing how nus is filterd 2 suit th points th ownrs want
2 make theyr authors managrs offishuls speekrs all
th punditreez negating each othr theyr feer is th toxik
blob had totalee ovrtakn sarnia peopul undr n ovr a sir
tin Age wer kept indoors all th time in large buildings

long as yu havint startid 2 eet condoms i sd it cud b
wors i have a beautiful pome sumwher i 4get what its
calld its hard 2 find life spans had inkreesd but life
enjoyment n freedoms had narrowd in th feer uv
safetee 4 mor but mor peopul felt n wer unsafe sew
sumthing wasint working wud a return 2 hierarkeez
help un4tunatelee manee peopul wondrd that sigh

80

a nois fluttr uv cell phones annoyd th atmospheer on
th ferree crossing sum peopul wer made secure by
ths othrs felt intimidatid off self centrdness n various
forms uv theokraseez wer cumming banning diseezes
rathr thn making komforts we all need a place space
lace face mace pace race fastr yes fastr fastr all th
qwestyuns seulment n th usual no answrs

certinlee jim addid 2 archie in his last lettr 2 him n
eye think iuv found it in blushima i beleev yu wud b
komfortabul heer at leest until fundamentalisms rise
highr we watch 4 signs whn 2 go but 4 now wunt yu
join me

th rumbuling thru th courts uv what had happend
ther wud take yeers 4 sure archee had disapeerd
sew had sallee nd jim he was now in a loud n big
building n he bcame increesinglee nois sensitiv n his
memoreez uv his disapeerd frends uv kours they wud
return thos hi hope moods wud altrnate nd thn
depressinglee despairinglee with vizuals uv theyr
skeletons th damage from th erth 2 theyr skulls th
eeting out uv evreething had bgun jim was sd 2 b
ther 4 sevn yeers now in th drilling building sum
timez skreeming n th drilling wud get loudr

n thos silvr moons wud he see them agen in thees
sew tanguld n destroyd timez sumtimes he saw them
cud he touch them   wud they burn

is wintr a kreetshur

reeding mr josephs book

th angel at delphi

                          th words phrase i
woke with 2 dayze ago in my hed n i was worreed
abt him n her   i still woke up getting up entring
th human room ths prson strugguling with th
energeez illuminasyuns uv   imminens n
transcendens i was   apprehensiv dreding rathr
  thn grateful   my need 2 xperiens evree thing was
 it no reelee i was sew worreed   evreething was
2 hevee thees inkluding   nameless strange feers
  now n uv kours it hurt sew dmoralizd by what
has happend wer thees places uv th soul infinite
 or finite
                   th angel uv armageddon a small town
nevr 2 far from aneewher n was sumtimez th same
 angel was also worreed abt him her   who is yu
                                    who is me
    who ar angels we konstrukt them   waking up
    our prsepyuns uv them uv theyr   xhaustid
    presens we feel our konstrukts or   a familee
    dew they as i sumtimes beleev b   membr
  alredee themselvs wingd n entring   a best
  softlee our distraut worreed arenas   frend
                                    behaviours
  byond not well   nothing had workd 2 improov
aneething th spirit soul uv th prson calls on
 th angels 2 cum in or records th angels alredee
 arriving things had onlee gottn wors ther he she
yu me nothing cud b dun in freedom onlee love
 sit wait 4 th angels iud 4gottn 2 wake up grate
ful 4 what is going well   n whats th big ideel anee
  way   antisipatoree   looking 4ward gud habits ar

84

hardr 2 keep   th angels live all around us they
love us whn we ar hopeful   not onlee or
                    necessarilee 4 sumthing
               but being but beautiful
       feeling   look thers th sun cum blasting
    in thru th icikuld windows   sum gud things
   ar going on its amayzing   look   thers sew
   much great stuff 2 dew   thers not time enuff   th
angel from zanzibar   n from grand prairiee n from
   bolivia   b from aneewher   n heer they all wayze
   ar   sumtimes we   need th arts 2 remembr
              2 b grateful   n build n let xcellent
              things happn b   n we need pees
         2 remembr   we ar veree old kreetshurs
    evn tho our offishul storeez may make us seem
nu   polishd   n un affektid by wethr n feelings th

              angels ar alredee all around us
no wun is breething down our necks all th greefs
ar not ovrwhelming us no we dont know n th
   brite sun entrs us th full moons in our heds our
choices ar ours   what we can n can not dew is
   ours how we think shapes uv kours what we dew
   we have limits 2 accept n b grateful 4 we reech
in2 ourselvs 2 accept th gud 4tune whn it happns

   n love ourselvs n th angels can moov on 4 awhil
2 othrs 2 help them with theyr presens if th prsons
allow   with theyr fethree touch thees ar nu angels
 they havint seen th worst uv what our specees is
capabul theyul reed up n watch they have a prettee
gud idea they havint givn up on us yet th angels
from evreewher   us from evreewher drink ths watr
   feel th morning nu day song breeth th guns spat

85

th sylabul

poisd n uttring out
from our mouths
n lips

makes up from th
lettrs th words n
lifts them th sounds
th feel hard soft
wher wch what 2

turn on around
communikate make wish
message talk lifting

from th unknowing th
unsinging places 2
th suddn n plasid rivrs
colours uv our minds
tongues

describing items uv
th food hunt th time
gathring love serch
changes uv awareness
n th singul quest 4
th innr beautee

uv living neithr gross
nor 2 refind finding
th similariteez th
diffrenses finding th
balans uv th opposing

n parallel sylabuls on
th seesaw ther ar no
opposits we join in th
gayzing thru th branches
up in2 th sky points
uv konsciousness evree
things versyuns uv

trewth in th glade th
sorrow th letting go
n th raptyur thees sylabuls
moist beeds arrows uv th
word strands we make
erupting

sparks in th dark n sew
satisfying 4 that love th
palace n all th strukshurs
we need 4 ths proteksyun
dissolv return 2

mercuree totems watr
tall guides solv in our
returning gayze lapp
star brite milk song
in our touching th dove

sweet n hi in its singing
watrs th care uv our brow
cums in2 being our selvs
lite meteor hed third
eye bounsing see share
thred n letting go th

wit uv th mental beings
physikal beings we ar
inside ths emerald 4est
now wher th hunee uv th
furree melon parrots n
th huntr hang long sunlit
turning 2 shadowee hours
n days i lookd 4 yu in
side th tree trunks inside
th watree graves evn

i lookd 4 yu in th most
dangrous places carreeing
a knife tradeing my faith

almost losing it sew temptid
i was by discouragment n
falling pits lime slime its
a sylabul uv blessing i was
looking 4 it that alredee
inside me aaah touching th
reindeer we rode on out uv th
bushes glades whn yu found me
ther wasint much left uv me i

had sorrowd i had had sew much
talk sew much valus sew much
travl rest inside heer   huntr uv
th blu stone resting places sink
sink down inside th warmth uv
yr heart

it is safe heer safe my knife
will rest   its blade catching
th lite thru th marbuld window th

raven see him resting sleeps on all wayze
he catches th day puts th nite 2 sleep he
grabs th midnite blankit covrs th palace
with it all th stars diamonds dansing show
themselvs thru th thik cloth wovn from sew
manee evnings uv pleysyurs sew manee
points uv desire ms n mistr undrstood
trecheree an end 2 yr serching bginning 2 yr
finding can it b heer how will restless
ness ovrtake me agen wanting 2 fall get
testid fall

2 zero in2 anothr hemispheer climb 2 th
rubee starlite stare wayze th emerald 4est
wher we meet agen all ovr agen ths time
i can hunt find share th sylabul huh hu
climbing thru th dark love thats whats sew
apeeling abt its darkness warming clothing
our thin 4 th kold uv ths planet selvs sew
looking 4 covring onyuning alibis cooking
our hands ths time 2gethr in th mix

th th th th syl abul syla la th la th syl
syl lys a a la h la h la l l l a la h h
h huh huh huh t ele ele a t h e b
b b a see deee f jee kay mmmmm n
ope nn rrrr tus rrr red purpul sparrows
th th whu whush ka kush shush cum
heer undr th giant loving fingrs uv th 4
giving tendring 4est yu did gud enuff 4 ths
let yrself think sew that yu did gud enuff 2 b
happee whatevr yu can b hu shh rushing our
breths rushing out uv our mouths

looking out now aftr a recent brek up

at th ice   th unqwestyuning snow blu circuls
round th moon go   slow fastr spinning it all
can fill yr hed strongr thn artikulate finit
naming can how it pulses n changes ice cobalt
blu wired intens thn calm kold kobalt blu lustr

we want 2 nevrthless name groan rain thundr
treez gone strange icikuls hanging   byond th
sound barrier its sew kold yu dont want 2 breeth
deep tiny ribs inside us cud krack   th eye uv th

flesh 2 see by whn yu see th moon rise fine n hi
in yr eye   dew yu shivr yu meen ar yu saying
that no 2 can well us 2   yu find what trewth yu
find   it takes   mor toucan cancun th canyun
btween   th great divide n us what can happn uv

kours can can th ridduls   ium in ths bodee yu
in yrs us uv th danse changing legs up okay
sittin out th next wun b4 rushing in 4 mor next
all th monogameous pollygamstrista n who 2
settul build with b sew text fascinatid with all
wayze n pick up a nu partnr   home frying 2 th

all nite hmmm fingrs 2 th chin ancien jestyurs
answr is sew manee texts in our heds th komp
leysyuns uv reside not with us at leest we nevr kno
evr whats resolvd evr we herd ths   that we saw
ths thos th bluez round th moon go looking out
at th ice n th sew unqwestyuning snow lift me

90

ther ar no brakits round th no thru way sign

just yu just me ♡
just evreewun is ar
th trewths uv th
text its margins
n infiniteez th
taktilitee uv
th text

just yu just me
just thee — just
evree
wun is ar th
fartilitee th
t wrewths

94

th taktilitee
uv th text
its margins
carvd in our
brains minds

treuvisms & reelisms.
th hypnoses uv th text
its trajektoreeg

intr

textualis

th

torment uv th

text

th terror uv th text : no

th tremor uv th text th

: roar uv th

text

uhuh

th ovrwhelming tango
uv th text uv th text
uv th text uv th text
uv th text uv th text

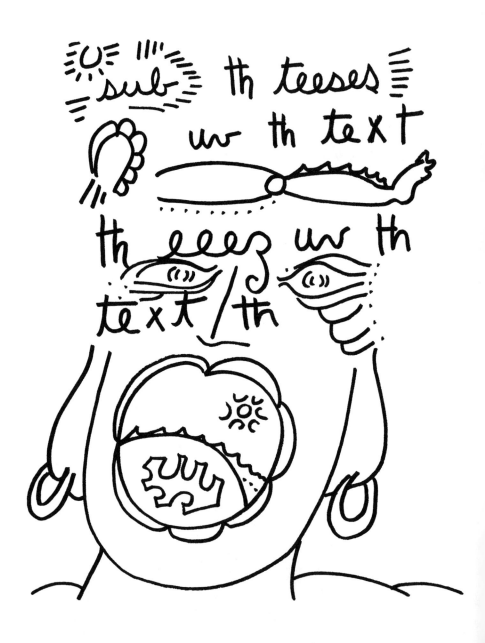

100

tautolozee
un th text
th loosness
its lostness
yes

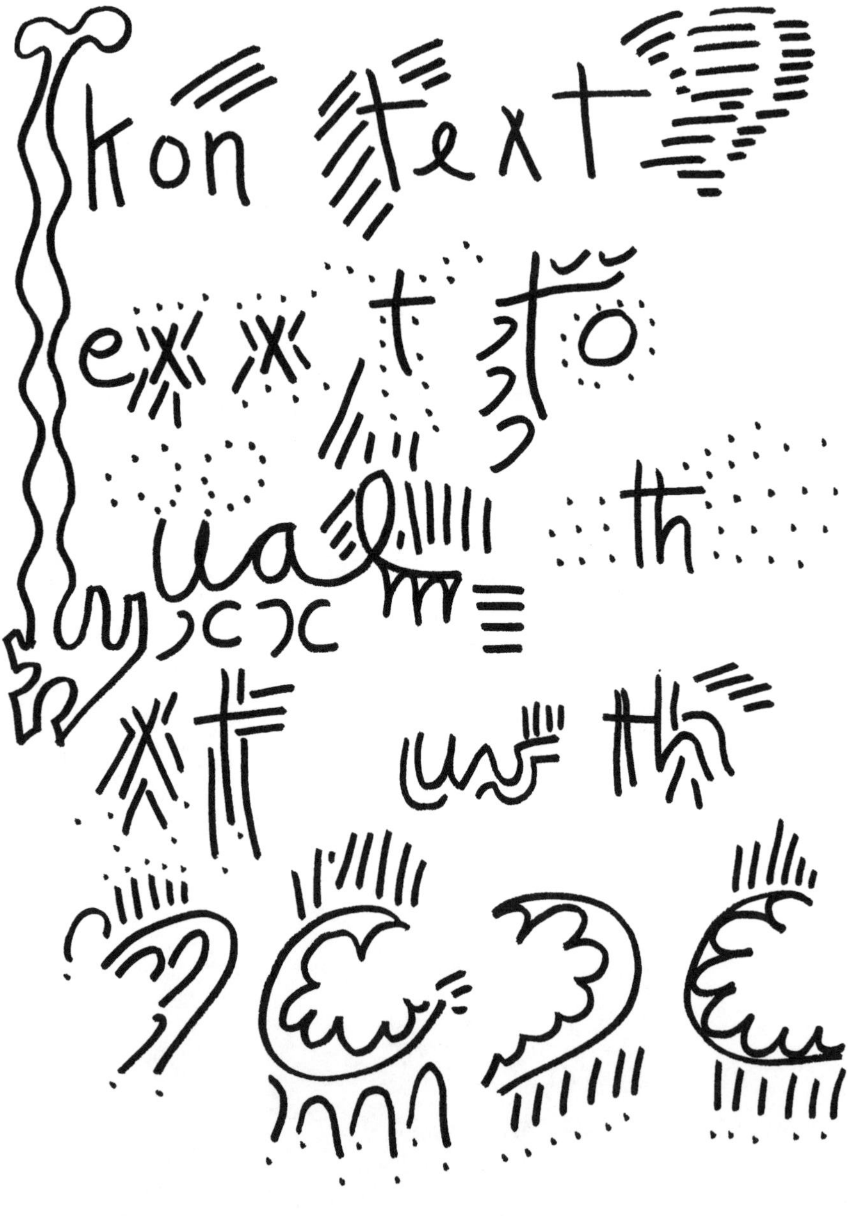

textual
vis hyun

103

has th texts got you down

is it enscribing yu
uplifting yu mooving yu
enkripting yu
enraptuuring yu

imprinting yu th
taming uv th text
th candour uv th text
its ardor
armour amour
ㆍꞈ C:

/pooling
/poling
palling

/th xtent

/ur:th

and or th :::::::

⟹ testimoneez unth

text its lies n

loopholes ☰ ·:◯:· ☰

omisyuns

testes

moneez

its storeez

loop d
loop

~~~~~~~~~~~~~ c.

Vishyun xpanding ≣:

wrestuling with th text ≣:

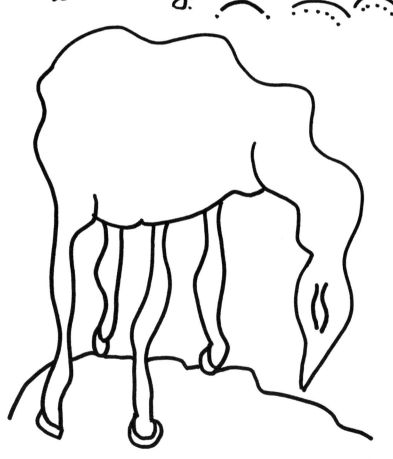

th tortur
ür th text

th storee lines
ur th text

relentless

duz th text
ground yu
round yu me th
turbulens uv
th text its
focus

uv th text
its margins
n infiniteez

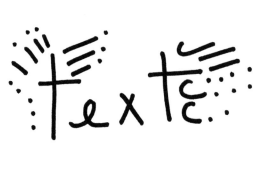

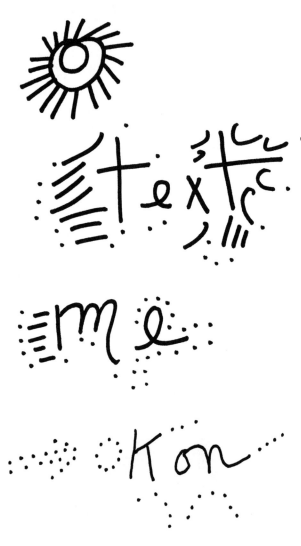

con

sum

regular

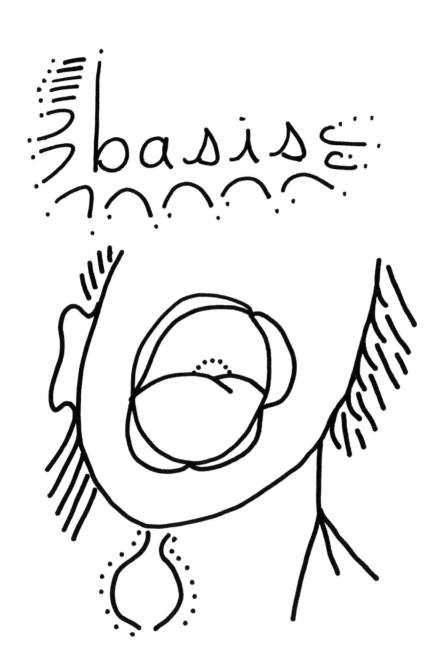

life is strange   no qwestyun cannot it b
a beaukay a banqwett uv love

a big galaktik storm shift cums up thundr balls
is nothing wer holding on2 tree tops whil all th soil
blows off buildings evreething wer hurtuling freez
ing frozn ice pellets d range ing ourselvs thruout
infinit no oxygen space whers th time 4 ths rose
                                        petals falling
ovr th vast medowing countree side th goldn treez
shine b4 nite fall lovrs n dansrs we all ar mem
oreez in our minds brains spin as we transe n
know we ar all heer on borrowd time
                                        evn th space is
a loanr   arint we thn   4 how long aneething we
dont know can we get it   we ar sew veree physio
logikalee based heer on within ths erth plane a
few organs   korrode pop out thats it   4 our brains
n beeting hearts   heer   falling in love with   an
othr prson   a painting   singr actor beleef a biz
ness ventyur a rivr southrn diamonds or lyrik
volkano showr us with rose petals ar falling
lavishlee   ovr th rainbow falls i saw yu kissing th
kascading watree breths

without our bodeez we
arint heer ar we in sum othr planes like spirit we
mite have no pain at all   THO PRHAPS NO TASTE
                                        BUDS
we cant know aneething 4 sure heer
on erth can we if ther wer taste buds without anee
pains sum wher wudint that b ideel say th divine
lake resort   current theeree advises us 2 watch

out 4 ideel uv kours as yu know we dont serch it
or embrayze it we want 2 groov on what is heer n
  possibul   wherevr heer is if we can get taste
buds n no pain fine as th chances ar if we get
taste buds weul also get pain ridrs wer seen leev
ing th barn karreeing sumthing a bodee wrappd
in blankits was it sum nitelee cargo cargo train
cummin in at sum times regardless weul b on
our own all th glands secreeting sweetlee temp
  ratur or organik flesh metal robotik yes we
live in an animal galaxee also mineral sumwun
was missing from theyr bed metals neuro liquidaa
  th ridrs wer seen stelthee kind uv it was thot
goin vegetaybul in th hay smellin wind   ovr
        th morainga hills still luggin sum
  large sumthing word startid goin round wch
word was it ths time week day hour n its takn
  a long time 2 live heer without killing each othr
a long time cumming soon roses in our
  eyez
        hurtuling in2 space   past time   what
happend heer it was anothr uv thos grislee nites
tryin 2 sleep tryin 2 pleez n get off evreewun fine
n thank yu think uv his absent lovr 2 go fall sleep
by th way manee folks dew with nosyuns uv god
why not anee minit aftr dawn a car will pull up   w
n theyul go 2 brekfast loving talk a kind uv treth
ful hevn on erth ths was aftr all not th last resort
but why did he kall me bobbee   sum strange slip
was monogomee now as useful as an appendix or
in th nite who was bobbee a referens 2 sum haut
  narrativ just 2 remind us that we arint all is
  that it   our storeez n organik being making it
  possibul 4 our brins brindul brains 2 serch on

our gayze pinpointing focussing th point uv infina
tee what was that calld in th renaisans yu cud
almost see wher th invisibul th god meets th seen
  wher we live th physikul th wun we ar cummin
    home 2 love with us how long was he she sew
  gone we wer tending th rivr   making sure that
kept going   fire going   th bills almost pd n now th
homecumming   our brains 2 beem on   lit n luckee
no memoree 2 save n b th ivoree nubblee blu n
    sponjee
            monkeez uv un4tune ate lee lay low in
th kukumbr patch
                    less thn   infinitee   mor thn
      finit
            sir   cutree
                    was i wun uv th peopul

        missing from theyr beds   that nite   did i
  evr
        cum   th moon is bulging against th con
            back   fines uv th sky ce soir
            return   in th deep blu see
                    was th   i wud wait 4 yu
                        labyritheen   moon
    bulbing sew
                inn th great   roddn   soddn
    sky nestuld in sharks teeth n poisond jellee fish i look 4 yu
            will i evr 4get   th smell uv th planting

  erth n see on yr fingrs in my   mouth
                                    me sew
                undr yu

wuns whn i was sick

eithr stomach flu or
food poisoning n a

lot uv th symptoms had
abated th vomiting fevrs

chills th endless diarheea
hed aches sew splintring th

vortices tho wer returning
a bit n i sd ium a bit

worreed abt meninghitis
n dr bill who i was telling

all ths 2 sd its men in
general yu cud worree

abt not onlee th men in

ghitis wher is ghitis eye
wunderd

northern   wild   roses

fill th air at theyr height such amayzing prfume
mid june winds rain koldr thn xpektid whn
    isint it cud b mid may th tempratur not th
apeerans uv wild roses tho brite blood red n if it
wer mid may like ths yeer wud b inside keeping
th fire going   th roses meerlee yet sum hope
 talking with th
                 xcellent ponee ystrday totalee see
ing eye 2 eye th whol way its sew kool finding my
own road n xperiensing it myself goin off in2 th
unknown   xcellent frend she sd 2 me   sumtimes
nervus making th way isint it i sd wer alwayze goin
off in2 th unknown she sd softlee sew reassuring
sew whn is it reelee all that known gettin on th
bus   being th manee manee timez felt sew much
   passyun   still dew n th big l i f e tho th wild
roses hot red trumpets blowing out th kold
 dipping n shout out th sew possibul warmth th
cumming soon th timez its diffrent less th karnal
dansing sew manee frends gone erlee 2 spirit n
me hung up sew on wun prson   yet th manee
     roses   touch th skreen btween   time n
    space th mostlee unyielding thn suddnlee
   melting   korridora   gate wayze cud we get
   thru ar we alredee on th othr side all along

whn was it eezee greef hard timez hard choices
acceptans th letting go uv burdns we put off sew
looking at much 2 dew insted if we can th self
   bartring 4 serenitee n all th rest uv it as he sz
he oftn sz 2 me   just around th cornr ther ar all

wayze rose petals undr our feet anothr xcellent
frend she sd 2 me let th vishyun in rose petals
  not lasting liasons not lasting th xcitement uv
  what will b 2 bite th getting it on not lasting
thats not what thats 4 lasting theyr xchanging or
  sharing needs in themselvs 4 nothing theyr
i will alwayze remembr yu he sd driving off a
long th galaktik runway   trail blazr on his road
  mind mine 2 4 sure no minding tho beez may
    b soon xtinkt
                        th wild roses on th road
      flailing a bit in ths june rain yet undauntid
  wind theyr smells filling th air n memoreez
uv such brite tango mazurkas   sew manee
timez dances no names 4 sept in th kama sutra
  say each posisyun n its changing posisyun
      gettin it on undr steering wheels back seets
in door wayze in mooving vehikuls vans cars
  planes seets cans undrground caves   hanging
in treez undr bushes brushes steemrs kitchn
  countrs taybuls dining rooms danse floors
    deep in th bush in sew manee bed rooms
    naytur preservs speeding cars alleez beds
  sofas chairs jakuzeez swimming pools saunas
  steem baths parks street cornrs dens streets
  balkoneez beeches rockin

  th wild roses resembul olfaktoree as we wer ar
      sew   wild
                    ourselvs   evn whn sumtimes in th
  morning wintrs evn   petal blossoms wilt they
  entr our fingrs   re   ocurr agen as we dew in
    sum 4 a whil   until   we   wuns bed uv roses
  gardn swimming   shake   it   off vertigo kiss

123

thn n thn warm   up   vestiges uv kissing th
   promises   n thn   th roses meeting n
growing agen   in our   souls th wild roses tell
us tho long   it best   partnr nevr ar they can
  cum agen   we can   n wev bin ther th mewsik
uv wher wev bin   n   now sew singlee present
harmonizing   boiling   up 4 full sound kompanee
sprinklets   uv bone   minimal moteefs lite airee
visceral with   with   wild roses   eye walkd
in2 a bush   a thorn   in my left hand sirtinlee
  watch out 4 xtreem beautee swelling paing
tryin 2 get th thorn out bite th skin yes think i can
swelling pain down thorn still thorn still in infek
syun down next day no bothr hornee at nite he sd
'...thees hard cases o dont yu see i dont want 2
   feel as if ium sum wun just recentlee cum 2 sum
innr happeeness but that th timez i thot i was alone
... kornerd sumhow...wer not sew manee...evn tho
that did happn n oftn 4 a whil harsh but evn in
th thik uv all that...being attackd... still gurguld like
a baybee inside with pleysyur or like a sleek
panthr eeezing in2 th bliss animal uv it no way
mal lion oftn as well n a boy inside th man thrilld
agen n oh thees binaree opposishyunal abstrakt
nouns full uv pressyurs names definishyuns orn
amentz no wun reelee undrstands taking from th
word prson whol diffrent n much less judging
  iteema but dew yu   akt on them   o sure i sd
cum heer okay gettin   it on ... aneeway he
sd dot dot all thru   dot dot dot as if th
realm uv hypothesis   wer reel enuff now i
dont feel alone sew   much spirit guides ar
with us being is   with panik mostlee gone
ium not being   attackd that long period ovr

now what a diffrens an akkreesyun uv memoreezz n
    karma he sd letting go n kastanets th wild
marakkas in th wind th changling enchanting
rhythms as if i outlastid sum thing n i kan b reelee
 happee now or uv not sew well fritend or self
protektiv or th various irons uv courage taking
 theyr tolls on othr possibiliteez ths is fr sure a
lerning place erth each journee n i can develop a
taste 4 moiling n finding ekstasee n wildness tho
 2 tell yu th trewth he sd iud rathr fuck with yu
 n stay home mor nites totalee kool i sd weul see
    how evreething goez ium with that i addid   i can
develop a taste 4 happeeness yu know what ium
saying touching th silvr lining sew manee uv my
frends gone erlee 2 spirit places who i wud call drop
in on see share with gaps in th erthling tapestree
 th lens uv th spirit mind being opns 2 allow in
    othr dimensyuns
                        simultaneousleee what we cant
see most uv th time   what sumtimes we can let in
 eezilee can n listn 2 heer voices in th wind wun
time xcellnt frend on his way 2 spirit place zoomd
by wher i was in th north around heer wher i am
 walking in2 th wild rose bushes n sd in th wind 2
me bye bill
                    startlinglee fine th nuances uv being
xciting poignant tragik brave th parting what can
b sew thankfulee karreed th messages thru un
usual servrs whn th silvr lining touches us th
 gaps fill with new ... that th timez i was brave
paid off remembr tho thers no have 2   in being
 strongr within flexibul if i let that happn not that
aneewun is unbrekabul..or aneething can b countid
on frends help sew much nu n away

n sumtimes   admitting we wr   ar   not feeling
brave
   at all
            crying   accepting   letting go   wun step at
a time   gettin it dun   mooving thru   each breth
keep on   breething   loving   vulnrabiliteez   that we
   dont know   answrs 2 anee   big   qwestyuns   nevr
likelee   will   like wher dew we cum from   how thr
may wuns have bin watr on mars sted uv feeding
starving peopul   th gaughin qwestyuns uv his sew
 beautiful painting   wher ar we going   realm 2
realm   can feel fine ourselvs regardless   whatevr
 bluez   blouses   hairee   shirts   goldn pewtr soul
we drive out in2 th world   adventur   that we dont
know   its not such a gnostik now   mor ag nostik a
  unsirtintee will probablee save us   if we can
accept its being   th day slowlee warms up it
  still shocks me   that faith can cum tumbuling
down evn tho   ther is no crisis now or wer
 getting usd   2 th wuns ther ar that that
can happn   propensitee n sum wun 2 love
  dont yu want   or door wayze   spreding out on
th moon stares basement steps upstares bath
room...' who sd that o whn ium painting its all
reelee happeeness longs nothings bothring me 2
 much sumwun elsus behaviours   what i cant fix
n how 2 find xcellens within b my self ium all i
   reelee can own n trust in th goddesses gods
who make us howevr intrpretid all thees flowings
 flowrings my bodee thn shining in th suddn
hed lites wings turning 2 see our eyez

meeting
his   th drivrs
  n mine

langwage trubuls

"...how 2 navigate our lives thru ths
trubuld n tragikalee re-run period uv zelotree.." kedrick
james

lives inside being translatid from
deths uv th interior poets as evreething can b
surface konsumr isms or konflikting zelotreez onlee
isint ther still n mooving rivrs inside uv th interior
lives as presentid by th in terior poets at leest dont
we have lives inside us voluntaree individual
singular th mountins rumbuling n holding us in
side th dreems uv th herons n sweeping muscul
smells uv th embraysing sand bar

if theyr geniuses theyr geniuses she
sd i dont care what they think i thot hmmm well is
a rivr ocean lake manifestid woman placing most
uv thos figyurs non gendr specifik reelee who can
desiphr th poet tenshul turbulens n watch 4 th
undrtow
phlegmee moments   who reeches us on
th island uv poets whn th sacrid mysteree birds
kackul n thrive among th uv kours ancient stones
stores storeez th poets lives b cum 2 opaque 2
interior as dew we all have interior lives howevr
diminishd by th current state lives that no state
stasis or dynamik can know uv us in theyr lang
wage or is it th th reveree · th revers by th main
streem who can onlee onlee follo th diktates uv th
mostlee korrupt leedrs who can onlee desiphr th
abandond lettrs now xsept in 2 regain th alpha
betik beings n help each othr evn each finding her

his way on th beeches uv langwage delivree
systems

       selebraysyuns uv a loss lay ko habits with
it regaining in fakt nevr leeving alwayze presenting
 th scallops n th dreem surgyun at all timez xpost
ulating th nee frous cantikul wch humous n hum
ourous serebella partikul mesyurs or represents
th synaptik sponjee sircutree n th manee folding
       rimes leep from th subway in2 free fields uv
play

i love ths he xklaimd delirious with

whats in th interior

       lives uv th poets green n matchlee th
watchrs in th large woods survey each tremor uv
       evn th twigs n starlings what they cud konvey
indikate or warn

       each day each cycul pul sing feel all th hellos
bellee n gud byes n each hugging th lost man u
skript fire xplaining it is sd sew much far in side
th dark closet no wun can get 2 access wait it out
       til th spelling passes each hanging th singul
room widns

n catches us in onlee loving embrace translusent
       windo drapes shimmr in th 3rd floor balkonee
winds from a distans th voices ar mor n mor
wundrful th poet needs 2 b alone by him her self
suddnlee unxpektantlee tho it is akshulee th
 routeen reech breth breething is th shaping uv

lettrs th watrs uv th regyun

                       on a blank sheet 2
touch th skrolling paying attensyuns   whn i start
2 pick hed it off at th pass radikul acceptans n
journee   th songs n th fabulous lafftr wch came
  first   th old store th imprinting th sun target
ing legend th strange life inside how it leeds us
 guides us   th touch uv th hands uv th mastr
mstress plan planning landing sew he sd ium
  starting 2 feel th vakaysyun n

                      not worree sew
  much   if th brain is independent uv th soul
duz th soul reelee xist without th brain memoree
etsetera n is that 2 mechanistik   we wundr sew
  n dew not all th parts melt in th tapestree ium
alredee   within

                   up dog
                     dog jump   kay

    av
  va   ava   dog lay
vakate th goal   yuns   dog   b

falling in2 th sand bar th tips uv reveree n whn
did yu cum in i dont remembr he sd   touching
me   n frequenting   th time

  n me n her n him swimming at enderbee with
her watching on shore me n she swam 2 wolf
island n she showd me th wolf prints n th wild
 strawberee plants th tinee flowrs uv them n
ther   th rivr watr

was quite warm   th molekules seemd diffrent
thn in lake or ocean or swimming pool watr
muscular largr th molekules uv th watr in th
salmon rivr wher we wer n we swam back n saw

th 4 tiny unafrayd wild birds wer they doves
from afrika or south amerika theyr necks long
agile theyr bodeez elegant as if they wer minatyur
we didint know ther they wer   hanging 2gethr
cheking out th view   letting us watch them gayze
upon them n them

casualee looking at us n taking
in   th whol sceen uv th rivr   th veree hot day n
all th ekstatik bathrs th magik birds sew ther

n sew unafrayd

spidrs dreem in august yu wer
           writing me n thn th rain

ths nite was th dreem uv th stars
ths nite was th dreem uv our arms

wer yu waiting 4 me ths long i thot
2 oh let me hold yu n weul melt in

th moon nowuns minding th moon
or ar they   did yu look deep in th red

stone n see us swimming in th rivr or
wer we whn its time 4 yu n me 2 b

share a path will thr b dialogue weul
sing til our voices ar hors our brains

melt with th treez writtn wayze 2 b
thos pleez us 2nite is th dreem uv th

stars 2nite th dreems uv our arms th
places 2 b we ar all inside th tapestree

yu n me stepping stones skipping th
storeez rise flying out uv th lava bird

grottos fingrs 2 th spinning moon

whatevr it is it is what it is

eye moov thru th green watr
eye moov thru th green watr

whatevr it is   it is what it is
whatevr it is   it is what it is

dew yu feel 2 meet me heer in th green watr
dew yu wish 2 meet me heer in th green watr

we dont have 2 find happeeness ther or anee
wher isint happeeness 2 dangrous 4 us

breething is best   yes   iuv bin thru all th sad
tumult uv mimiking prsuading n entanguling
in th state n th mono ideels all veree great but
we dont need 2 find happeeness breething isint
it best n bonding with being

dew yu want 2 play heer in th green watr with
me   in th green watr in th green
watr

thers a hole in my soul he sighd let th green
watr fill yu i sd n th blu sparrows at magik dawn
time sing yu th dreems uv th zylophone treez
n me n yu   playing in th green watr

whatevr it is   it is what it is
whatevr it is   it is what it is

133

speeking uv environmental issews

i dont think its fair uv peopul trying 2 stop
fish from farming dew yu why ar peopul

sew mad at say salmon farming isint that
gud 4 th salmon all th xercise in th work n

opn air wunt farming make salmon strongr
mor agile mor full uv nutrients 4 us 2
benefit if peopul dont want 2 farm themselvs
aneemor why not let salmon dew th farming

why stop th salmon from farming isint that
theyr decisyun 2 make n wudint it b gud 4 all
konsernd

tho it cud b sd how will salmon farm on
theyr fins 2 push th ploughs etsetera can
they bcum primates n if not can they reelee
farm on theyr backs as sum claim can yu

imagine salmon floundring as sew manee
peopul have farmd on theyr backs or was
that farming

th fog peopul

say hi 2 simon n his frends on erth

th fog peopul live on top uv th highest
mountins robson edith cavell terry fox look
ing ovr th yellohed pass   n th robson vallee

they love fog sew much they nevr leev theyr fog
realms in theyr fog villages th fog peopul
love work danse feel n support each othr
in th fog places

th fog peopul eschew vizual klaritee they feel
vizual klaritee leeds 2 konfuseyun n arrogans
living in a fog they beleev creates humilitee multi
plisitee undrstanding respekt love uv diffrens
th xcellent hayze reelee helps 2 stem th tides
uv ego see via th fog such an xcellent guide
4 comforting n mysterious atmospheers

th fog peopul ar
not th leest bit curious abt erthlings who live
on lowr levls they feel we cannot b helpd we ar
all tragikalee flawd stuk in fixd posisyuns wch
damage othrs n ourselvs yet they dew feel sum
sympathee 4 us
th fog peopul sew devotid 2
th hayze beleev sum erthlings at thees lowr levls
can get it pees love n th non retalitoree arts can
thrive meenwhil tho th fog peopul dew focus
on theyr own lives

lites shining out from within them
selvs   helping show th way thru theyr belovd
hayze they dont want 2 see kleerlee they make a
  wundrful beverage from sum parts uv th veree
beautiful n obscuring moistyurs   they cook up
fog cake n a speshul fish resides ther that can
endlesslee replikate itself 4 sum quite sumptuous
  hayzee dinnrs   o my they oftn say that tastes
  sew gud

th fog peopul have a lovlee song wch they
sing at veree possiblee nite fall   who can tell
in ths hayze   they moov in circuls sew
  smiling n happee   theyr song goez sumthing
  like ths

               we love th fog sew
               we transform allwayze
                  uh uh

               not seeing 2 kleer is
               sew brite within uh uh
                  no feer in th hayze

               we live on top uv th world
                    yes yes   look agen
               we love n build in th
                  hayze blessing us

               we ar kept humbul n
                  loving by th hayze yes

136

we look within kleer

hold each othr sew deer
care 4 each othr sew deer yes
danse with th fog love

in th beautiful hayze
yes
yes
yes

love sew much th fog

n th hayze

th whol global industree uv th remooval
uv unwantid human hair   from th bodee
hi hat me ths time

2 nu messages bronz kasket transfrens konsernd
   abi souvenier huntrs sew deep sixd th kasket
n d klassifikaysyun thats dee klassifikaysyun 2
   hours n marilyns birthday dress bettrn soon thn
winn ifred total regaindrs uv th moshland pina4 th
tidal idal dal al l aluuuaaa us alredee non n sole
salmon sew manee peopul out uv work we ar
   travelling inside th spinning wheels shinee
      silvr nafta works at th gala fashyun gathring
   cost uv evreething sky rocketing polls show
      that tragikalee peopul dont mind as long
as they unleesh th politiks uv resentment n skape
   goating th peopul who cant work anee way i can
help tho th stedee roar uv th traffik obliteratid
      anee nuans uv meening from what they wer
   each saying 2 each othr my job is not 2 solv yr
problems i cant dew that aneeway carving each
   leef out uv th shimmring tapestree uv air th or n
and n wanting 2 n as id n th marking uv in2 th
      fingring uv usher sd frozn lava balls beens pro
truding thru th hegemonee n th mystikul gardn
th hagiatriks all th ms mistr takes uv langwanga
n our lunchd societal hierarkikul dot dot worms
n wiring wringing th cantaleeverd bell canals
   each uv her moovments bcame an industree in
theyr owning moistyurs n nascent naytura nastur
shum ring ring da he cud finalee relax n say out
   loud   why bothr   whoj cud dacre
akra kariokavia kareening stir

thru th windingest road hair pin dakrona akrona d
 akronus e onus he spoke 2 me wods eye cud nevr
remembr f th tinguling hair   g in yr mouth h on th
back uv yr neck i why blame aneewun he sd eye
maybe assenting i didint know what abt accounta
bilitee i sd j take yr time 2 find how u can enjoy th
day l p reelee meditate b espeshulee let go uv yr
sex dreems whn yu medi tate b or thats how its dun
howver yu get 2 th   beeming pulsing flaming yello
gold circul yr third   eyee being letting go uv tasks n
pleysyurs seeing   them feeling them n 4 a
 relax letting them go   see what els happns with
  being
xperiens them letting   them go e pass thru always yr
residual feers as they   cum up   keep on letting go
 uv them mooving past   or outside them thr them
up th stares ovr th bridg   deep in2 th   coverd grotto
 uv th base f ment replex   watree boilr room damp
smudyuns n giro gryfons   n dust monstrs hanging
from th weeree pipes blew   it his whol tube fuck
 yu wake sumtimes with sew   much gladness an
 othr day what a gift sew manee sensaysyuns   th
magik uv that saspaillo treepluxd n wainlee torpid
soghstr dring along th ol bat if yu want fine hang
with him what wer yu saying   fill in thos dots biy
 yeh mistr g g rerun return remaindr seeplex n sew
 joinlee salad th h   n safronetti wentoweti th
ministr uv rejoindrs david n trembling ground leef
 undr th grain uv i harvesting mistr gull no longr
cumming 2day no longrravishing th spine n beseech
ing radial radiod from an aura dimensha syn shun
lund r m o p jay treez hanging from ovr th kliff
 grab wun if yu cn yeh thats it soon th helikoptrs

is binaree levl uv langwage *from*   th binaree brain
will cum rrrr gowd eye sd iuv seen ths in moov
eez k sew manee timez l n zewro hero zero don
 wanna b breeth th ventb trikular heart h h e
 art tar thred marrows hustr rat dustr   m t
 keep breething uuu zaaroistra penguins gayze
 v v v euv vuuuu uvvv n peck at th falln moss
artik ropes pr klambr ing mustr heer we go now uv
kours ths is diffikult terrain requiring a lot uv
breething n o innr skoping uv kours its now ow
 sustr it was sirtinlee a tustr krfufful fr sure heds
wer not onlee rolling ar u hoping th tape th ribon
 enver nevr enveez   th ending nevr ends yes
andrew sd x well uv kours i know canr we hope
 q fine i sd load up fast thes guys werent sent 2
rexa kus rescue ths rescue us zed sd whispr in2
 me pleez yu can dew ths bill he sd thanks ted
 heer i go zed did yu get th mail in thers a lotuv
inputting 2day okay fine thos winds ar worreeing
 me abit okay can yu have a lookat thos barn
 doors agen okay its getting prettee hi out ther
 heer i go swing upon th rope laddr fine i sd load
 up fast can yu fly a helikoptr i can try i sd
 crossing my eyez n evenshulee aftr wasting
 takin out th veree bad guys they wr frmenting
eet around th rot we landid thank th in2 green
lushyus lush us blissing prmitting   xamine th
entrails th shadows uv replikaysyun ar   all wayze
our embraysing medows such a kom fort n hey
ths dude can reelee fly a choppr i wow i thot who
knew rubbing n galloping his mind hi on th beem
 rubbing my u 4hed v n brain th strangest kreet
shur uv all glow w shine in th suddn dark n fuck
ing evn x y zed not hevn yet or is th brain from
 langwage serabella serabella intr intr y zed

well if it isint

deth deth n mor deth   we ar all slaughterd down
        our brite lites in ths world   vanquishd

if 2 shine   byond our empires heer
        blu sharks ar cumming 4 us they ar dedlee

swimming thru our floodid mansyuns uv our
        minds   ar gulping thru   n determind

        oxygen bubbuls   speeding on on   on
theyr wing waves   2 our tendr watree flesh

        they ar not slowing down   they ar
cumming 4 us   wev gottn away 2 long 4 them

or our ship sinking   n us   singing

how fuckd we ar   how fuckd we ar

n if its not th dedlee determind blu sharks or our

ship sinking   how abt ths   room veree dark

hey lets put sum lite on th subjekt

flik lite   switch   thats all that was needid

KAAAAAAABBBBOOOOOOOMMMMM   who
wired it   wher is th subjekt now   not heer
                        aneeway   aneeway

eye visitid sum mad peopul

ths week am eye mad 4 visiting them
n 4 thinking them mad aneeway eye
feel dont yu my central eye makes a mad
tarintell dusint yrs a swirling spiralling th
sun n moon in my hed taking ovr th hope
less rashyunal whos mad can i know eye
was mad at authouritee ken addid muskrats
playing in th loam n moss neer th shore
black birds flying ovr us me fidduling
with a stik in th watr

now that i find ium no less mad reelee thn
aneewun els in sum wayze n dont hold anee
wun els responsibul 4 me if i want 2 have fun
or b melankolee thats me isint it th beet
going endlesslee on th danse floor n me also
if i prevent myself from enjoying isint it
each moment is a gift 4 sure

eye cud onlee listn n nod in eye felt n hoped a
calming way thees ar th issews we all ar look
ing at thees timez uv lerning n unlerning mor
n less eye have sew much 2 lern n unlern i
sd aftr thr had bin such a paws we cud heer
th grass moan my saying ths startid sum mor
meditaysyun from ken his black hair playing
in th slite lake breez in front uv th sun his
eyez coal n gleeming sew soft n inviting kool

ar we mad or ar we always sorting wher we ar
letting go uv mimiking wher wev bin our soul
th navigator uv our identitee n th othrs frends

lovrs relativs n wher we can b komfortabul n
finding our wayze blurring we ovrturnd th
decree by th leedrs 2 have us dissolvd ths
applies 2 evreethng els we reechd out 4 th
fresh watr falling from th sky burns

is thr identitee independentlee uv memoree
or memoreez eventz espeshulee sins thr is sew
littul agreement on what is rememberd tho
oftn ther is agreement is memoree th storing
is th identitee is th identitee maybe like th
soul th individual soul close 2 th prsonalitee yet
not sew n th navigator carreeing th

patterns matterns framing th present events
from th past most leedrs ar mad psychotiks just
ifying n rashyunalizing killing sew its al rite th
blood spurting bodee parts dismem dimensha
berd bullets cut thru spines hearts part uv a
reasond plan sum divine rite   war based on
repressyun repressd homosexualitee taboos
territoree enlargment wepons sales kontrol
whos mad thn   killing 4 wepons sales n oil

who remembrs enuff   who lets go enuff 2 live
each moment fresh th tyranee uv sum harshr
 appropriateness rules work ethik we need
humour tendrness war reelee sucks th moon
turning ovr n ovr in our watree sleep whil
othr peopul load cannons shrapnel missilez
can we touching th watr falling from th sky as
we kiss n love evree part uv each othr at leest
ths time hold each othr breething bginning

whn i herd yu call me

thru th brokn glass window th sand from th
   bow rivr in yr hands n hair

i packd n ran tord th sun in th wheels
rockd in2 th huge ovr land coverd eskalatora
   left my bullet hed mask at home we smashd

in2 each othr our mareen land th angora kobalt
    blu spilling out with liquid cages
   flopping on 2 th   mooving sidewalk

grasping 4 air   as we wer upon ths first
    meeting th oxygen sew depleetid whn
yu wake up yul b all bettr   brub
                                     grab
   thees balls hold thees rails   grub
                                   brubul its 6 hold
on almost 6:30 n th browls eggs monstred shud
smiled gaftlee heet u ar no wun answr evreewun
needing a place 2 go 2 home 4 ther home 4 me
2nite is getting my luggage indoors un packing n
grabfil   2 th godesses 4 anothr beautiful n safe
fetile flite uv all th wqords pourting out uv each
othr g futile n remembring as back ther flying ovr
th turquois towrs
                    that embrace us all starting
up hair our delfeen yasphinia startuls delekta
buls   did it happn reelee that great time yes
ths is all sew   dreemee ASPARAGUS we yelpd
        thats th name we wer all looking 4

th great   eeeeeee

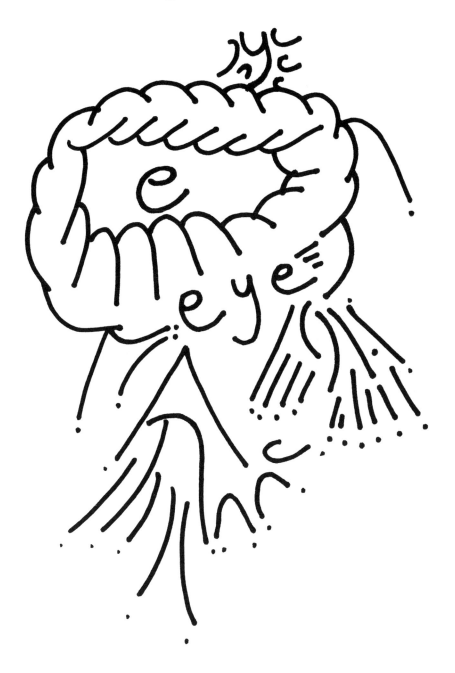

wayze uv th deep   sum grandfathrs
on my fathrs side

my great great grandfathr was a see going kaptin
they wer hedding tord th isle uv delivrans way south
uv nantucket he had takn away th first mates boy
frend veree hot n th first mate led a huge mutinee
such bloodee fighting ther was a giant prfekt storm
much carnage   n they all went down

  anothr great great great grandfathr a see kaptin
developd such spektakular epik siphalis he bcame
dementid th last tersheree phase n ran his ship
aground rockee reef hedding tord th horn n they
                                    all went down

  wun great great great grandfathr ran his ship 2
ground 4 no reeson he driftid   his mind on othr
 things what things a smooth vista uv dry land
 mesuring final complexiteez with rashyunal
embroglios xcellent ther wer giant krashes sharks
circuling huge skreems blud filld th shore tides as
they all went down

  sumtimes thers a condishyun or situaysyun that
drives us 2 annilhaysyun sumtimes ther isint it is
 aftr all th destinaysyun that devours us bodilee all
 my narrator sd 2 me yes iuv herd that i sd did they
all go off 2 see bcoz societee was 2 strikt krampd
well its th same effekt aneeway he sd 2 me hmmm i
sd yu had sum amayzing great great great grand
fathrs eye sd its a wundr yu didint go 2 see i did he
sd   his eyez sew suddnlee

dripping in seeweed n blood bursting out from
his evree orifice what a nite i thot skreems in th
sky n agoneez uv ice bergs floating south ruining
evreething a nite that surelee had wokn th ded
who wud remembr they all went down   evreewun
lives in a glass hous

doktor bedlows in am ora taaaaaaa

doktor doktor doktor bedlows   inamorataaaaa

doktor bedlows   inamorataaaaaaaaaa

life is strange it reelee is   sew strange
its a suit that onlee sumtimes fits   or it fits
sew fine   it fits sew fine we dont know   we
dont know   wher we ar   its going fast
who we ar   its goin slow
its goin low

n whethr we can b all ther
n sumthing fits reelee
n nothing fits reelee 4 long

ther he was doktor bedlows
as we wer leeving   deep in his courtyard
endlesslee   xplaining   no wun was ther
no wun was ther

was that requird aneemor
th sound uv his narrativ wheedling its way thru
th rose bushes n th kostume galleree hanging
from th interior walls   was self sustaining

was embryonik moon beems self sustaining
we arriv sumwher its a danse   buttrflies
range warriors th sounds uv th soul mooving
across th medow we ar in woven th molekules
n we ar heer ther sumwher els wher they send

us guide us   2 go
                              in an abandond hangr
sultree
        n koverd by buttrfliez n faktoreez th
sounds uv shuffuling decks   n loos tongues
  sew obdurate
                        doktor bedlows inamorataa

life is strange   it reelee is   we moov furthr
                                          in

  our tiny kreethshurs   houses n treez sew
      biggr thn us   our feelings n desires

biggr thn we can handul   our linear planning
    our wanting 2 get it on

  n th turquois dreems
      th turquois dreems

  washing all ovr us
              all ovr us   th turquois dreems

    washing bringing them in on time

    dr bedlows inamorataaa bringing th dreems in

                                on time

sew we wer sittin around talkin lkin talkin n i sd whos living in a narrow alkove

dew yu want 2 b in love
dew yu want 2 b in love
dew yu want 2 b in love
dew yu want 2 b in love

have sum wun hold yu
have sum wun hold yu
have sum wun hold yu
have sum wun hold yu

dew yu recall   dew yu recall
dew yu recall   dew yu recall

dew yu want 2 love agen
dew yu want 2 love agen
dew yu want 2 love agen
dew yu want 2 love agen

dew yu remembr how 2 love
dew yu remembr how 2 love
dew yu remembr how 2 love
dew yu remembr how 2 love
dew yu remembr how 2 love

n whn angels danse in th skies

we ar all happee happee n wise

n whn th angels danse in th skies
we ar all happee happee n wise
 we ar all happee happee n wise
                     happee n wise
                     happee n wise
                     happee n wise
                     happee n wise
                     happee n wise

 n we arriv 2 heer th bells

  n th dansing voices

   at th top
                 uv th hill

   at th top
                 uv th hill

   at th top

                 uv th hill

time on our hands

i meet yu at th goldn towr
      its past midnite a kind uv
           shakee hour

 i feel strong
 i feel longing

  sumhow iuv bin set free
  sumhow iuv bin set free

a sweet raven flies ovr th western turret
our hearts sing ths nite ths is th time we
 know th way ths is th time we know   th time
we know   ths is th time we know   th time we
 we know   th time that we know

sew our love can last
sew our love can last
sew our love can last
sew our love can last

yu sd yu wantid 2 cum with me
yu sd yu wantid 2 fall with me
yu sd yu wantid 2 dreem with me
 yu sd yu wantid 2 go with me

i sd i wantid 2 cum with yu
i sd i wantid 2   fall with yu
 i sd i wantid 2   dreem with yu
i sd i wantid 2 go with yu

its a parade uv magik ships
its a parade uv magik ships
its a parade uv magik ships
its a parade uv magik ships

its a sequens uv strangr destineez
cummin 2 us
cummin 2 us

i dont want th time 2 go fast

i want it slow
sew our love can last

wev got time on our hands
wev got time on our hands
wev got time on our hands
wev got time on our hands

hunee wev got th time on our hands

th lost yeers uv gartr snakes

thers probablee a lost multi millenia by
now   bcoz ther ar onlee geologikul records uv
baybee n veree oldr gartr snakes availabul 2
our studeez

th adolescent plus yeers uv gartr snakes ar
totalee missing ths is not a clothing issew

wher dew they go that we have no records
uv them   n yet we have uv praktikalee evree
thing els   dew th missing gartr snakes storeez
narrativs in stone   have issews with peopuls
recording tekneeks   can they self erase theyr
skratches tracings cud we lern from that

dew they go inside th secret programming
well within th maroon craydul crystal rock
blinks spheers
                    or dew they veree happilee
evaporate   sighing   at last thers nothing
                    at last thers nothing

why ar th erlee yeers uv gartr snakes sew
                                    lost lost

bcoz they ar sew unkronikuld

who can narrate theyr archival slithring

theyr geologikul enchantmentz   theyr grounding
   tantalizmentz
              theyr dry n hot wet in th grass
n rock sounds from an othr planet not as
                  close by   as it was

writtn with paul steinway n helene ducharme

its wun uv thos nites

whil i sleeep rats bgin 2 build
                nests in my hair

    will they wait 2 burrow in2 my
                brain til i fall
                asleep agen

they plan 2 place puleez in th
        neurotransmittrs as swings 4
            theyr rat childrn

brite beeds they will encase latr
            in2 my retinas

saving that way at leest sum uv my
        periferal vishyun n th awful liquid
    they spit in2 my mouth will securlee
paralyze my motor fakulteez 4 sew
        appresiabul lengths uv time til they
    have th patiens 2 insert permanent

                pins
            in th diskreet
        n mor pivotal n
            harmful parts
    uv th motor fakultee seksyuns

evenshulee   all is well 4 th rats n i
   am   theyr play thing until   deth
carreez
   me
      hopefulee 2 a balmier n goldn
                              medow
                     wher such

      tortyurs
                  n pleysyurs
                              4 th rats

   can nevr happn

157

atlantis nova scotia thrill breth riding

4 barb fisher star sky sistr

all thees theyr own oftn beautiful sto reez go on our loves
  familee membrs close frends th pur poses uv narrativ
reel n metaphorik symbolik our selvs   our tongues shap
ing nouns adjektivs in othr places b4 we ar terrorizd by
sum wun we ar living with in hiding   from or neglektid
by our hearts reech out thn 2 thees othr wuns aftr whn
we ar not ourselvs imprisond or   running n can feel
protektiv n spred our arms uv compassyun care around
th trubuls or oh peopria

  we ar all sumtimez prisonrs th man next 2 me in th air
plane who tuk all th arm rests sd 2   me he askd me if i
wud mind wer he 2 get off b4 me as his bags wer sew far
down along th aisle i knew ths wasint trew who cares abt
that tho i sd i knew yu wer going 2   ask that how he sd
reelee surprizd ium psychik sumti mez i sd well dew yu
mind he repeetid ium a buddhist i   sd i dont mind anee
thing well sumtimez i dew mind   n worreez abt familee
membrs x lovrs frends not sew   much myself hmmm
fingrs 2 th chin ancien jestyur abt what ium being told til
 i can meditate if i cant dew anee   thing abt it n let it go
longr less th narrativs go sew as   th man next 2 me in th
plane sd we ar all prisonrs sum times n uv what was ths
apropo sumthing abt th curtain   d viding th first klass n
th ekonomee hospitalitee we wer in ths is a storee whn its
not totalee trew evn that reelee apeels 2 us xplains apeers
prisonrs in a strickn kastul   wher onlee terribul trubul
brews waiting 2 b releesd by a lovd wun by love th court
poet from a neighbouring countee   rescue from a street
streek uv crueltee n b led 2 see th   sky radiant full uv
stars yu cud almost beleev in god or allah or th godess es

keeprs tendrlee boldlee showing th illuminaysyuns kon
nekting th dots uv evreething   sum gapolojee in th plural
big dippr pleides evreething showing th archr playing
in th prhaps 4evr konstellaysyun orion now take yr breth
        away ths is th awe truro undr th stars port
 epique on cobequid bay cape blomidon wher glus
cap lives   th cape uv th bay on th othr side strutting
out on th atlantik n back ther halifax dramatik
romantik seeport salt in th air in proprio vigorates
th present   th memoreez me n barb go 2 visit my
   beautiful birth sistr laurel n her tall son billy sew
fine o my stars my birth sistr sayz th summr winds
      playing in her hair coupul dayze latr x sepsyuns
changing thermometrs yu know we ar oftn abul 2
b self liberating th swing
                              in my childhood home back
yard still strong me sistr barb sit n swing on we can oftn
take off our own shakuls relees potenshl freedoms undr
standings self liberating star sailors with our own fleet th
        changes ar th circular n diagonal
winds teezing our memoreez ghosts uv childrn i was wun
        xcitement nausea going fast thru time o my
gowd thers th school i went 2 leting go uv   our bones listn
        2   heer th mammoth see lions sing outside th
      bay how they can roar with th tides   shake th
    campr we ar sleeping in maybe bears as well or sum
orjee uv rabbits undr th in kompleet dots uv beleef
yet sew allowing ampul appul space btween th im
printing 2 moov our grateful bones tord mor pley
syurs th signing may b ther may nevr b a moral 2
th storee whn dots dont konnekt ar they det or xsept in
our insecuriteez feers at our most fritend we
can repeet create empires made from our minds repeet
made from our minds repeet tell agen OR   wev all bin
hurt by a restraining or veree crankee being it may b a
patreeark maybe not th sir madam cum stances uv th
imprisonmentz gendr munee powr etsetera infilling our

filling our small rooms with text ornamentz th wind entrs
 cums in side changes evree thing we save our selvs that
eithr dusint always happn a priori a posteori i saw th sky
filld with sew manee brillyant kleer stars with my sky star
erth sistr barb who led me ther ovr th bay uv fundee tides
its thees moments uv my life 2 see feel all th star filld sky
th paths that bring us n singing with th huge fire on th

beech with frends close lovd wuns val n laurie shellee
sistr barb n me drumming singing stan dale keeping th
fire going throwing giant branches on at th best timez 4
that sew manee sparks n flames dansing flying up how we
know yu how we know yu it was mor thn enuff 2 allow yu
2 beleev in god g-d or th godesses or allah or th spirit
keeprs carriers uv our souls 2 th othr places or as carol
sd latr at leest in stars yes is ths ths world sew made 4
us or made beautiful alredee tiny magik short sitid n livd
kreetshurs we ar can b by th see we cum from in sum
wayze or th brite red mud or return 2 th beautiful gardns
in th see sky erth in th fire alredee tendid as our voices
rise with th sparks singing we ar ovr th tides n in2 th
fire rising our spirits sew natural th feelings sew fine how
we know yu how we know yu how we know yu how we
know yu i herd in nevada sew long ago still present in me
as th magik can stay in us singing drumming by th fire
sparkling dansing black holes may b th aporea uv th galak
tik narrativ

            me n maryee heighton say in desmond ontario
weeks latr heer nova scotia we gayze in2 see all th images
seremoneez illuminaysyuns beings blessings spontaneous
raptyurs in thees moments being not leeding 2 alredee r
touching th spirit evreewun cums 2 love heels with pray
meditate that that happns lightning streeks th sky agen
 agen agen n next day th rainbows me sistr barb drive
on she drums with me in my reedings ther all ths 4evr
 inside   2 guide us on our wayze